GHOSTS OF
CAMBRIDGE

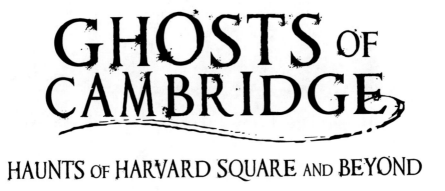

GHOSTS OF CAMBRIDGE

HAUNTS OF HARVARD SQUARE AND BEYOND

SAM BALTRUSIS

Published by Haunted America
A Division of The History Press
Charleston, SC 29403
www.historypress.net

Copyright © 2013 by Sam Baltrusis
All rights reserved

Front cover: Memorial Hall, which is allegedly haunted by a Civil War–era soldier. *Photo by Ryan Miner.*
Back cover: Dunster Hall and Ralph Waldo Emerson plaque confirming that "Cambridge at any time is full of ghosts." *Photo by Ryan Miner.*

First published 2013

Manufactured in the United States

ISBN 978.1.60949.947.1

Library of Congress CIP data applied for.

CONTENTS

ACKNOWLEDGEMENTS

Thanks to my spirit squad from Cambridge Haunts, including Ashley Shakespeare, Nick Cox and Hank Fay, for helping me rouse the dead and give a voice to those long departed. The ghost tour helped shape the tone and lore featured in *Ghosts of Cambridge*. Ryan Miner, the book's photographer, deserves a special shout-out for working the graveyard shift and capturing Cambridge's spooky, old-school aesthetic. Major thanks to the handful of paranormal investigators and researchers who helped make *Ghosts of Cambridge* a reality, including Adam Berry from *Ghost Hunters*, Gavin W. Kleespies from the Cambridge Historical Society, master psychic and East Coast medium Denise Fix, Joe "Jiggy" Webb from *Paranormal Hood*, MaryLee Trettenero from Spirits of Charlestown and archivist Christine Wirth from the Longfellow House. I would like to thank Andrew Warburton, my eagle-eyed Agent Scully and research assistant, who helped uncover some of the skeletal secrets featured in this monstrous project. Thanks to my mother, Deborah Hughes Dutcher, for being there when I need her most and my friend Joe Keville for his continued support. My co-workers at Scout Magazines, including office manager Melinda LaCourse, deserve a supernatural slap on the back for their understanding while I simultaneously managed two magazines, including *Scout Cambridge*, and burned the midnight oil to write this book. I would also like to thank Jeff Saraceno from The History Press for his understanding approach to *dead*lines and his support during the process of putting this book together.

Introduction

I've spent my whole life chasing ghosts. My earliest memory is of my biological father's house in Chicago's South Side on a street called Loveland. My maternal grandfather, visiting from the Florida panhandle, set up a lawn chair in the front yard and just sat there for hours, gazing into the horizon, which included a red-white-and-blue water tower with the town's name etched in bold letters. My grandfather was a kindhearted man with salt-and-pepper hair and black, '50s-era glasses. My parents were fighting inside. I ran into the front yard to be close to him. He smiled at me.

A few months later, he passed. However, the serenity in that man's face has stayed with me for years. My mom, with long, Cher-like black hair, received the call that her father was in the hospital, dying from complications associated with diabetes. She was in tears, crouching on the floor and trying to shield me from the news. I was four years old.

My parents divorced, and we moved to Florida. We stayed in my late grandfather's house in a neighborhood called Avondale, and I had what would be my first encounter with a spirit. It was him, my grandfather, and he was smiling. After his passing, my mom said she felt his presence one night when she was home alone. An unseen force touched her hand to let her know everything was going to be OK. My mom knew it was her father but was too afraid. I never forgot.

He's been with me over the years. Sometimes he shows up in my dreams, sitting in that chair with a familiar gaze. He usually doesn't say much, but I know that he's there. Then I wake up.

When I was younger, I believed in spirits. The first book I remember reading was *Gus Was a Friendly Ghost* by Jane Thayer. I checked it out of the library many times, and I would spend late nights in bed thinking about the history and mystery associated with the spirit realm. Ghosts were good.

As I started to develop intellectually, my theory was challenged. I repressed the initial encounter with my grandfather and spent most of my young adult life wearing "paranormal blinders," or shrugging off the possibility that ghosts do, in fact, exist. I turned it off…but not for long.

I had my first spirited encounter as an adult while living in Somerville's Ball Square in the early 1990s. I recall seeing an apparition of a young girl who would play hide-and-seek in the hallway. She was a mischievous poltergeist, and I remember hearing phantom footsteps leading to our second-floor apartment.

Since returning to Somerville in 2007, I've spent years investigating alleged accounts of paranormal activity at sites all over New England. I've collected a slew of reports from these supposedly haunted locales, and the mission was to give readers a contemporary take on the bevy of site-specific legends. *Ghosts of Cambridge* is, in essence, a supernatural-themed travel guide written with a historical lens. Based on my research, the city is a hotbed of paranormal activity.

While digging up these tales from the crypt for my first book, *Ghosts of Boston: Haunts of the Hub*, I started spending hours in Cambridge's Old Burying Ground. I've always felt a strong magnetic pull to the dead man's dumping ground—which boasts Harvard presidents and African American soldiers from the Revolutionary War—and I was interested in the subterranean Vassall tomb reportedly located beneath what was known as "God's Acre." One night, when I was setting up for a meeting at First Parish Church, I had a close encounter with an unseen force. The back door, which was oddly propped open by one of the cemetery's old-school gravestones, mysteriously closed. I heard what sounded like the floorboards creaking and then a second door slammed shut. I looked up and spotted something, or someone, out of the corner of my eye. He looked like a Revolutionary War–era soldier, and he was wearing a tricorn hat. I held my breath.

At this point, I didn't know about the legend surrounding Lieutenant Richard Brown, a British soldier who was shot in the face in 1777 by a Patriot sentry while descending Prospect Hill in Somerville. He was buried in the Vassall tomb and allegedly haunts Christ Church, which also abuts the Old Burying Ground. Apparently, his interment was so controversial that hundreds of crazed colonists ransacked the historic

Where's Waldo? A featured stop on the Cambridge Haunts ghost tour is Harvard's hallowed Meyer Gate. The hidden plaque spotlights alum Ralph Waldo Emerson's spirited quote: "Cambridge at any time is full of ghosts." *Photo by Ryan Miner.*

Anglican church. Brown's spirit reportedly comes up, slams doors and blows out candles.

Was my encounter at the church a ghost? Not sure. However, I do believe in residual hauntings or a videotape-like replay of a traumatic event that occurred years ago. My theory is that Cambridge's Old Burying Ground is full of skeletal secrets, an energy vortex of unjust killings and unmarked graves dating back to the days leading up to the Revolutionary War.

A few months after the incident, I decided to launch a ghost tour based on the Harvard-centric research that didn't make it into my first book. The historical-based Cambridge Haunts romp through the city's darker side was a hit, and I quickly met the spirits along the way. Ashley Shakespeare, a friend and featured performer at Jacques Cabaret, became the tour's lead guide and resident ghost magnet. We had several spirited evenings walking through Harvard Yard. We stumbled on a plaque hidden behind Harvard's Meyer Gate quoting alum Ralph Waldo Emerson. It read, "Cambridge at any time is full of ghosts." Boy, was he right.

During an early run-through, we spotted what looked like a full-bodied apparition peeking out the door at Memorial Hall. After chatting with locals, we learned that the Gothic structure commemorating the 136 Harvard men who died fighting in the Civil War oddly didn't memorialize its Southern alums. After one guest on the tour snapped a photo of what looked like a Confederate soldier with period garb and facial hair, Shakespeare and I were both convinced that the legendary ghost of Memorial Hall is a Southern gent who left to fight for the Confederacy during the winter break in 1860. The soldier has made a postmortem return to finish his education.

While writing *Ghosts of Cambridge*, I've uncovered some historical inaccuracies tied to a few of the city's ghostly legends. For example, one of Harvard's dormitory haunts, Thayer Hall, was supposedly a textile mill at one point and even made Hollowed Hill's *Haunted New England Colleges* list in 2009. According to the website, spirits wearing Victorian-era clothing were spotted entering and leaving the building through doors that no longer exist. Not true. Despite the retelling of the myth, which includes several mentions in other books on the paranormal, Thayer Hall wasn't a textile mill. Many legends—like William Austin's Peter Rugg literary character, who stubbornly rode his horse into a thunderstorm in 1770 and was cursed to drive his carriage until the end of time—didn't exist. However, people over the years have reportedly spotted the ghostly man with his daughter by his side frantically trying to make the trek back home.

For many, the only real ghosts that exist are the ones that haunt the insides of their heads.

In the last few days writing this book, I was mysteriously drawn to the oldest structure in the city, the Cooper-Frost-Austin House on Linnaean Street. It's open once a year, in June, and my intuition led me to the little white building tucked away in North Cambridge's Avon Hill. The lean-to "half house" was built by Samuel Cooper, a deacon of First Church in the early eighteenth century, and was passed down the Cooper family tree for 250 years.

The historic home is near Cambridge's public execution place, known as Gallows Hill, where hundreds of people were executed, including an African American slave known as Phillis, who was burned at the stake in 1755 for allegedly poisoning Charlestown merchant Captain John Codman.

However, the supposed spirit haunting the home passed in 1885. According to Brian Powell, a house resident and tour guide, he's heard several stories from former tenants who claim the ghost of the last owner, Susan Austin, still lingers in the upstairs bedroom. "I was checking out a book at the Boston Public Library and the librarian recognized my address

The Cooper-Frost-Austin House, the oldest building in Cambridge, located at 21 Linnaean Street in Avon Hill, is a stone's throw to the site of the city's public execution place, known as Gallows Hill. Built in 1681, the oldest building in Cambridge is rumored to be haunted by its last owner, Susan Austin, who passed in 1885. *Photo by Ryan Miner.*

as the Cooper-Frost-Austin House. He said that he lived here for a week and would never go back," Powell recalled.

Why? "He said it was haunted. He was literally spooked and spent a week in this house in complete terror. People speculate it's the last owner, Susan Austin, but I've never encountered her," Powell said, joking that he's comfortable sharing a home with the female specter. "I don't care if she's here. You can be dead as long as you don't bother me when I'm sleeping," he said with a laugh. "But I've been approached by psychics and others who believe the house is active."

As far as my face-to-face encounter at the oldest building in Cambridge, I did catch what looked like a shadow figure dart across the downstairs in the main hall, which boasts original masonry detail in the fireplaces and the foot of the structure's chimney dating back to 1681. During the tour, a hanging lamp mysteriously started to sway when we were in the original kitchen area, and when our small group toured the allegedly haunted upstairs bedroom, oddly in a state of arrested decay, we heard inexplicable phantom footsteps creaking above us in the attic. Apparently, the third floor is where the servants stayed. In the past, I've spotted what looked like a full-bodied apparition of a woman, lit by candlelight, peeking from the window of the second-floor bedroom when I've walked down Linnaean Street.

Was it a spirit? Perhaps. I do know that somewhere deep in my subconscious, ghost stories satiate a primitive desire to know that life exists after death. The truth is out there.

GHOST DIARIES

While writing *Ghosts of Cambridge*, I fled my room with a "boo!" in Somerville's Davis Square. The house's resident spirit, a playful older female poltergeist with an affinity for scissors, did various things in the house to make her presence known. According to a psychic who visited the two-floor Gothic-decorated haunt, she was a seamstress during the Depression era. While I was writing my first book, *Ghosts of Boston*, an unseen force opened doors that were firmly shut, and lights mysteriously turned on and off without provocation. One night, I spotted a full-bodied apparition of a gray-haired female figure wearing an old-school white nightgown and donning fuzzy slippers dart across the first floor while I stood, in shock, at the top of the stairs.

The ghostly incidents escalated after the initial encounter. While I was preparing for the launch party for my first book at Boston's Old South Meeting House, the scissors sitting on the front-room table mysteriously started to spin, and one night, during an interview with *Paranormal State*'s Ryan Buell's Paranormal Insider Radio, I heard a loud knock on my bedroom door. I quickly opened it, but no one was there. Oddly, the phantom knocking continued throughout the phone interview. I wasn't afraid.

Months after I submitted the manuscript for *Ghosts of Boston*, a construction crew was hired to paint the exterior of the house. Apparently, the spirit I called "Scissor Sister" didn't like the ruckus outside. What was supposed to be a month-long project turned into more than a year. The first crew of painters claimed that paint brushes would disappear and ladders would fall. One guy, tormented by a series of inexplicable incidents, asked me if the place was haunted. I sheepishly nodded, and I never saw him again. After a series of freaked-out painters, scaffolding from the top floor fell on my roommate's car.

The jig was up. I decided to move.

Master psychic Denise Fix picked up on the spirit of the seamstress during our second interview. "She's not trying to scare you. She wants your attention," Fix said, sitting at a table that, oddly, was a repurposed Singer sewing machine. "She sewed for many people and felt quite tortured a lot of the time. She was celebrated by you, and she thanks you for that. She was released from whatever bound her there," Fix continued. "And it wasn't a good thing to be bound there."

Two weeks later, I moved out. My last night in the house was memorable. My roommate's exotic parrot escaped from its cage and perched on the oven's open flame. The bird was quickly engulfed in flames but didn't catch fire. The bird was unharmed. While carrying boxes down the stairs, I slipped. I felt something hold me back as I watched the box fall down the stairs. Glass shattered. It could have been me. I fled the haunted house on Hall Avenue and haven't looked back.

The search continues. The motley crew of paranormal personalities featured in the book's "Ghost Diaries" introduction helped fuel my journalistic drive to leave no gravestone unturned and give a voice to the ghosts of Cambridge still lingering in the shadows of the city's haunted landscape.

GAVIN W. KLEESPIES, CAMBRIDGE HISTORICAL SOCIETY

When it comes to Cambridge's tumultuous three-hundred-year history, fact is stranger than fiction. Gavin W. Kleespies, executive director of the Cambridge Historical Society, was quick to point out the many skeletons from the city's not-so-Puritanical past. "I would be hesitant to say that Cambridge was more progressive back then," he said during a recent tour of the historic Hooper-Lee-Nichols House on Brattle Street. "You have people like Cotton Mather coming out of Cambridge and then heading off to Salem during the witch hysteria. His father, Increase Mather, was a Puritan leader and administrator at Harvard. They both accused innocent people of witchcraft and then sent them to prison, and some of them were held in Cambridge."

Apparently, "the prison was atrocious" and housed many women, including Goody Elizabeth Kendall, who were wrongly accused of witchcraft. Kendall was believed to be executed at Gallows Hill, in North Cambridge, during the seventeenth-century hysteria. Kleespies, a Cambridge native who returned to his hometown in 2008 after earning a master's degree at the University of Chicago, said the city didn't become a center for progressive thought until the late eighteenth century. "Puritan New England was horrifying in many ways," he continued. "I wouldn't say there was a blood lust, but there was definitely a callousness back then."

Newtowne, which was the original name of Cambridge, was founded on September 30, 1630, when the deputy governor of the Massachusetts Bay Company, Thomas Dudley, was on the hunt for a "fit place for a fortified town." He convinced John Winthrop, the first governor of the colony, that the land surrounding present-day Harvard Square was an ideal spot. "Newtowne didn't last that long as the state capital," Kleespies said. "Cambridge didn't quite know what to do for a long time until 1636, when Harvard was founded. It gave Cambridge an economic purpose, and it quickly became the place to go to college in colonial America."

Kleespies said early Cambridge was a typical Puritan New England village town for almost a century. "By the mid-1730s, Cambridge started developing as a resort with country estates for wealthy merchants from Boston. The way to get from Boston to Cambridge was over the Great Bridge, and it wasn't something they could do on foot in a short period of time. So these country estates for wealthy merchants were built, and it slowly became Tory Row."

As anti-British sentiment started to escalate, Cambridge became an unlikely hot spot in the days leading up to the Revolutionary War.

Gavin W. Kleespies, executive director of the Cambridge Historical Society, said Cambridge's not-so-Puritanical past boasted a motley crew of witches, rakes and rogues. *Photo by Ryan Miner.*

George Washington, who stayed in Cambridge for almost one year, assumed his role as the leader of the troops on July 3, 1775. British general John Burgoyne, who retreated with troops after losing the Battle of Saratoga in 1777, was held prisoner in Cambridge. Apparently, the British soldiers weren't treated well.

"One of the officers from the Convention Troops was shot in the face and killed because he didn't stop when a sentry told him to," said Kleespies, alluding to the spirit of Lieutenant Richard Brown, who allegedly haunts Christ Church. "When he had his funeral at the church, the townspeople ransacked it. I mean, it was a funeral. They were supposed to be given proper quarters, and the officers were European gentlemen and they weren't expecting to be sleeping in a pub."

Burgoyne spent several less-than-stellar nights at the Blue Anchor Tavern in Winthrop Square before convincing Cambridge's leaders to move him into the more plush Apthorp House. "As far as the treatment of their prisoners of war, Cambridge has a really bad reputation," continued Kleespies. "It was shocking. These soldiers were expecting to be treated with a certain degree of civility, and they were thrown out in the street. And then a Patriot shot one of their members in the face. Unbelievable."

And then there was Gallows Hill. Kleespies said it's likely hundreds were killed at the public execution place, which is now a private parking lot known as Stone Court, located near 15–19 Lancaster Street in Avon Hill. "One of the last legal burnings was in Cambridge," he said, referring to Phillis and Mark, two slaves accused of poisoning Captain John Codman, in 1755. Mark was put into a cage to decompose near the current Holiday Inn on Somerville's Washington Street as a public reminder of his crime. Paul Revere, who rode past twenty years later, mentioned it in his accounts of his midnight ride. Phillis, on the other hand, was savagely burned at the stake. "There was some really gory stuff at Gallows Hill. Some nasty stuff happened there."

With all this Puritan-era tragedy, are there ghosts? Kleespies, who lived in the historic Hooper-Lee-Nichols House in the early '90s, said he was originally convinced. "I don't know if it was because I was a lot younger and impressionable, but if you asked me back then I would have said, without hesitation, that this place is definitely haunted," he said. "Creepy stuff happened. Doors opened and closed. Objects would mysteriously move to different locations. If you were here by yourself, you would hear noises."

However, Kleespies has become more of a skeptic since his return to Cambridge in 2008. "All of these houses on Tory Row are extremely old, and very bad things happened in all of them. As far as this house, it's pushing 330 years, and lots of people have died here," he said, referring to the Hooper-Lee-Nichols House. "Is it haunted? I don't know."

Denise Fix, East Coast Medium

For Denise Fix, talking to dead people is just another day on the job. The master psychic and East Coast medium recently trekked through Cambridge's Old Burying Ground and chatted up some guy in the cemetery. "He's a fresh one," she said, draping her scarf over an old-school gravestone. "I was immediately drawn to him for some reason." The man's name? Seth Hastings. Unlike the other fellas gathered around her at the Harvard Square haunt, her new friend is six feet under. Hastings passed on October 15, 1775.

Fix, who has been channeling the spirits for twenty-five years, said Hastings was eager to talk and told her he was cold. "That's why I put my scarf on his gravestone," she said with a laugh. "We were just goofing around."

As far as tapping into the spirit realm, Fix said it's a gift she's had since childhood. "I do see dead people," she said later during a sit-down interview at Somerville's Center for the Arts at the Armory building on Highland Avenue. "But they reveal themselves in different ways. Sometimes I can see them in my head and sometimes I can physically see them. However, they usually come to me as apparitions. Like, I can see right through them. But then, they throw you off guard, and they materialize and stand right in front of me."

Denise Fix, master psychic and East Coast medium, connected with the spirit of Seth Hastings, a colonial-era man who passed on October 15, 1775, during a recent tour of Cambridge's Old Burial Ground. *Photo by Ryan Miner.*

And Fix said she's able to connect with the disembodied voices from beyond. Based on the medium's interaction at Cambridge's Old Burying Ground, Hastings was a talker. "There's seeing and then you can sometimes hear them. Sometimes they're jokesters. They'll knock on a door or do things to get your attention. They make the lights go out or make the floor creak. They do that."

The medium said there's significance to the year Hastings passed, in October 1775, and the residual energy lingering in Harvard Square is somehow tied to the Revolutionary War. "Some of the spirits around us are wearing uniforms," she said at the burial ground. "There's a lot of residual energy associated with men from George Washington's era. I keep seeing men wearing [tricorn] hats."

Hastings's message from beyond? "There's no such thing as death," Fix mused. "Your energy changes and the spirit lives on," she said, adding that his postmortem words tap into her philosophy as a master psychic. "I love teaching people that there's something else out there. Life doesn't end, it just changes. My goal is to let people know that the energy lives on. There's no such thing as death. It's just transition."

Fix, a regular on the *Pat Whitley Restaurant Show* circuit and featured expert on paranormal-related TV shows, said the residual energy in Cambridge reminds her of her hometown, a certain North Shore hot spot known for its witch-trial hysteria. "As far as spirit energy, Salem and Cambridge are very similar. It's the same stories but different players."

It was in Salem that Fix had her first encounter with the supernatural. "I was five or six when it first started," she recalled. "I couldn't go to sleep at night, and my mother wanted to know why, and I told her about the kids in my room. She thought it was a nightmare, but I knew it was something else."

Fix said her childhood was like a scene from Stephen King's *It* or *The Shining*. "These kids would appear, and they wanted me to go to a party," she explained. "In my head, I knew if I went to a party with them, I wasn't coming back. And then the ghost kids were like, 'If you don't go to the party, we'll get your sister to go.' So I jumped on my sister to protect her, and she woke up screaming, saying I attacked her. My family thought I was nuts."

As far as the creepy Armory building in Somerville, Fix said it's not haunted in the traditional sense. "There are things that go through this building, but it's not haunted by anything from the past. But spirits are everywhere…there's energy everywhere. There are spirits who visit here," she continued. "For example, there's an old woman who used to work here. It looks like it was an office and she was in control of the paperwork here. She's no longer alive, but she's still in the building."

Fix started chatting up the lady spirit who allegedly entered into the room. "There was a business here and she was in control of the business," she said. "There were some kind of records kept here." Built in 1903 by George A. Moore, the Highland Avenue structure housed the Somerville Light Infantry of the Massachusetts Volunteer militia and then the national guard. For years, the building stood vacant.

"A shadow figure just darted behind the curtain," she said. "Sometimes they materialize as shadows. You can tell it's a female shape, but you can't tell much about what they looked like."

An article in the now-defunct *Boston Phoenix* alluded to the Armory's lack of paranormal activity. "The labyrinthine basement of the Somerville Armory really should be haunted," wrote Camille Dodero in 2005. "After all, it's a cobwebby maze of narrow tunnels, creaky staircases and exposed-brick walls that look like military catacombs pillaged during an invasion. There is a corroded group shower, a shadowy ammo stockroom with two empty vaults, and a firing range with bullet dents forming ghostly figures on a dead-end back wall." Apparently, photographer Pia Schachter agreed with Fix about the lack of spirits at the Armory. "If anyone should know if this place is haunted, it would be me," she said while photographing the massive structure when it was in a state of arrested decay. "I was ghost hunting and really expecting to find dead bodies and I didn't find one."

If you're looking for dead bodies, said Fix, check the nearby cemeteries in Cambridge and Somerville. "There have been killings at different cemeteries around here," she claimed. "Like they physically got killed at the cemetery and buried and their spirit is still there."

While there's no way to verify Fix's claims, it's a scream to watch her do her thing. When she channels a ghost, her physical presence changes. "When I connect with a spirit, the energy shifts and I get goose bumps," she explained. "My whole body right now is one big goose bump. I can literally sit with anybody and go anywhere. But I can shut it off."

Think Whoopi Goldberg's character Oda Mae Brown in the 1990s flick *Ghost*.

There are many skeletons in the city's closet, Fix claimed. However, the ghosts of Cambridge want their stories to be told. "It's my job to give a voice to those who are no longer with us," she said. "Sometimes they just want a little attention," she added, alluding to the spirit she encountered in Cambridge's Old Burying Ground. "Seth probably hasn't talked to a living person in years. He was a flirty old man."

JOE "JIGGY" WEBB, *PARANORMAL HOOD*

When Cambridge's spirits speak, paranormal investigator Joe "Jiggy" Webb listens. In fact, his ragtag team of ghost hunters, including local videographer and *Paranormal Hood* TV and radio-show producer Marlon Orozco, make a concerted effort to give a voice to those historically marginalized in the major-network mainstream dominated by shows like Syfy's *Ghost Hunters* and *Deep South Paranormal*.

Webb's critique? Enough already with the same old formulaic haunts.

"The problem with these shows is that they do the same thing," he said during a recent visit to Cambridge's Old Burying Ground. "They go to the same places. We know that the Lizzie Borden house is probably haunted. Why do they keep going there? There's got to be a million other places throughout the country with a lot of history."

The forty-three-year-old paranormal investigator said there's a lack of diversity at these allegedly haunted locales and little to no representation of people of color on ghost-hunting TV shows. "Here in New England, we have so much history," he remarked. "You can't tell me that all of that history is outside of Roxbury, Dorchester and Mattapan." But most investigations he's seen focus on "white men with money," he added.

As far as Cambridge, Webb said he wants to leave no gravestone unturned when he investigates an allegedly haunted location. "It's a beautiful city," Webb said. "It's very diverse. I grew up in the South End and would come into Harvard Square all the time, and I was interested in the history here."

Webb said he had his first face-to-face encounter with a ghost when he was seven years old. He saw a full-bodied apparition of a man who introduced

Who you gonna call? Joe "Jiggy" Webb, lead paranormal investigator and mastermind behind *Paranormal Hood*, wants to give a voice to those traditionally marginalized, like people of color, on paranormal-themed TV shows like Syfy's *Ghost Hunters*. *Photo by Ryan Miner.*

himself and then disappeared. "It wasn't like it was a reflection in a mirror," he recalled. "Clearly, it was like somebody standing right in front of me." The investigator said he later recognized the spirit from a photograph: it was his grandfather, who passed away before Webb was born.

"It was definitely him," he insisted. "I mean, my house in the South End was haunted. My house in Brockton was also haunted to the point that everyone in my family knew it was haunted."

Webb said his interest in the paranormal rekindled after a series of near-death experiences, or "NDEs," as he calls them. "I was always into it, but it just seemed so abnormal," he said. In 2003, he was shot in the leg and then walked away from a totaled car with just a bruise. However, it was his recent brush with mortality in 2006 that opened his so-called third eye. "I had a brain aneurysm that burst, and I ended up having brain surgery," he said. "It was extremely profound. It was so profound that I came back a different person. My beliefs, my understanding, my thought processes weren't the same."

Webb, who operates a security firm during the day, said he immersed himself in all things paranormal after the surgery. "People think you're crazy when you start talking outside of the box," he mused. "But when your brain explodes and you're trying to explain it to somebody else, it isn't the easiest thing. So I started coming out of my shell and began talking to people about it."

In 2011, he organized a team of paranormal investigators called HooDeez. Webb then launched an online radio show, *Paranormal Hood*, which included a series of TV webisodes chronicling the team's investigations at sites like Somerville's Prospect Hill. "I started reaching out to people who didn't think I was crazy, and then we started doing investigations," he said, adding that he's currently shopping around his own ghost-hunting TV show. "On many investigations, strangers walk up to us and participate. You can sit at home and watch these investigations or you can do them yourself," he continued.

Webb's plan of attack? "They always go to the same places and do the same things on these shows," he said. "Branch out. Do something original. There are so many things out there that haven't been explored."

The ghost hunter said it's important to embrace diversity and to investigate alleged hauntings in communities of color. "What we talk about to ourselves and what we talk about to other people are two different things," he said, referring to the African American culture. "When you bring somebody from the outside, they're probably not going to talk. We like getting the public involved. We like turning skeptics into believers. People are like, 'We don't believe in ghosts,' and then they completely change their minds after going on an investigation with us. It's the thrill of the hunt."

During the day, Webb has worked as a bodyguard for stars like Faith Evans, Naughty by Nature and Gavin DeGraw. When asked if ghost hunting is like chasing celebrities, he laughed. "I don't chase celebrities. I bodyguard them," he quipped. "I've met very few celebrities who are nice. So if you want to liken them to ghosts, there are bad ghosts and there are bad celebrities. If you're chasing celebrities, you're chasing something you want. I don't want to come back as a ghost. I don't want to haunt my family."

As far as local investigations, Webb said he was creeped out during a recent tour of Somerville's Prospect Hill. "I've been on many investigations, and this one definitely spooked me," he says, referring to a scene from the *Paranormal Hood* show where he's standing in front of the historic castle and feels something from beyond touch him. "It could have been a bug, but something makes me jump. I felt like something grabbed me."

However, Webb said he's less spooked when it comes to the supernatural and more wary of the living. "I've been shot and I've been stabbed. That was all done by living people," he concluded. "Ghosts don't scare me. People scare me."

MARYLEE TRETTENERO, SPIRITS OF CHARLESTOWN

MaryLee Trettenero sees dead people. However, she's flipped the script of the whole *The Sixth Sense* thing by reading the psychic imprints left behind at various historic locations scattered throughout New England. The intuitive behind Spirits of Charlestown taps into the lingering residual energy at an allegedly haunted locale and then channels the earth-bound spirits.

Dead man walking? Yep, Trettenero said there are ghosts o' plenty walking the hallowed paths of Harvard Yard. "I see people who are long gone walking, and many of them don't know they've passed," she said during an impromptu trek to Harvard's Widener Library. "I feel really heavy right now, and I keep seeing graves, as if dead bodies are buried around here."

Trettenero, who moved to Charlestown in the 1980s, said it was on the steps of Widener while taking classes at Harvard Extension that she decided to leave the hotel industry and become a full-time psychic medium. "I haven't told many people this, but this is where I made the decision to go into the business," she said. "Once I left working in hotels, it was the only thing that really interested me. I started at a good time because it's so difficult now. The [psychic field] has become so competitive."

In 2005, Trettenero decided to redirect her intuitive abilities and channel the residual energy at historic locations. "My premise is if I can read people, then I should be able to go to a place and read the land," she said. "If energy from a historic event is strong, it stays there." As far as reading an allegedly haunted locale, Trettenero said it's a two-fold process. "First, I pick up on the residual historical energy. The second thing is if there is spirit energy there, I would pick up on the spirits," she explained, adding that "it was a big experiment. I didn't know if it was going to work."

Trettenero said her first attempt at reading residual energy was at City Square Park in nearby Charlestown. "I sat in the middle of the foundation of stones, and I started picking up on slave girls," she recalled. "I got dialogue and what it was like working back then and what it was like dealing with the proprietors. So I would visit the site, do some protection and then tune in. Another time, I picked up on a bartender, and one time I picked up on a pirate. After reading a place, I go back and do research and find that it's often so true to form. I'm finding that what I get from the fragments I pick up at a site is historically accurate. It fits."

City Square Park in Charlestown, which was originally called Market Square, dates back to 1629. Governor John Winthrop and his crew of one thousand English settlers originally set up shop there before sniffing around

Standing on the steps of Harvard's Widener Library, medium MaryLee Trettenero taps into the lingering residual energy at an allegedly haunted locale and then channels the spirits. *Photo by Ryan Miner.*

Cambridge and ultimately Boston. Thomas Graves, an English engineer, mapped out Charlestown and built Winthrop's quarters, called the Great House, in the area before relocating to Boston's Shawmut Peninsula in 1630. Apparently, Charlestown lacked a proper water source. On June 17, 1775, the square was destroyed when British cannon fire burned Charlestown to the ground. Trettenero said she tapped into a residual energy lingering at City Square Park that predates the Battle of Bunker Hill fire.

"So when I picked up on the slave girls, I researched the slavery background and John Winthrop moving to Charlestown, and I found that slavery was totally integrated into society," she explained. "The last owner before City Square Park was burned to the ground was a slave owner."

Trettenero said she sometimes picks up on ghosts while researching historical sites. "A few days ago, I was at the Warren Tavern having lunch," she said, referring to an allegedly haunted watering hole in Charlestown built in 1780. "I was with a friend, chit chatting, and all of a sudden the lights started flickering behind me. She makes me stop talking and asks, 'Who is that?' I stopped what I was doing and tuned into it. I could see somebody wearing a black coat and he was severe looking. I immediately knew who it was—it was Daniel Webster. As soon as I said his name, my friend who is a colleague said that his name popped up in her mind as well."

How does Trettenero differentiate among the various spirits she encounters during investigations? "I have a sketch artist who works with me," she explained, adding that she first encountered Daniel Webster's spirit at the Bunker Hill Monument. "We do sketches of the spirits we see, and that's why I know what he looks like."

Trettenero started to assemble her residual-energy readings into a book format. In 2012, she launched a ghost tour called the Spirits of Charlestown based on her research. "About two years ago, I put it in the format of a book, but I put it down because it wasn't in a language that was easy to edit. I then added layers, like adding a sketch artist, and then I started working on paranormal investigations."

As far as ties to Cambridge, Trettenero said there's some overlapping with Charlestown because of its geographic proximity. "A lot of my stuff is related to the American Revolution," she said. "I know that George Washington was headquartered in Cambridge. I do know that the guy Harvard is named after, John Harvard, his original home is one of the sites that I do in Charlestown. It's not there anymore, but what I found is that it was a medical staging area. I just picked up on dialogue around it regarding clean water and arguments about who they are going to treat, specifically wounded British soldiers and people of color. Charlestown was burned to the ground during the Revolutionary War. But I strongly believe the medical staging was there before the war because there was a lot of violence before the Battle of Bunker Hill."

When it comes to her work as a psychic medium, Trettenero said TV shows like TLC's *Long Island Medium* with Theresa Caputo have catapulted the profession into the spotlight. "We all like her," she quipped. "It's when they break the rules. With Theresa Caputo, a big part of her show is that she goes up randomly and reads the guy at the pizza shop or somebody on the street. We always say you can't do that. You always have to get permission to read someone."

However, Trettenero said she believes Caputo is the real deal. "When they aren't breaking a rule, it's fine," she remarked about pop-culture psychics. "Everybody works hard to make the profession credible, so you hold your colleagues to a pretty high standard so they don't send us back to the Dark Ages."

ASHLEY SHAKESPEARE, CAMBRIDGE HAUNTS

Forget *Ghost Adventures*. Touring with Ashley Shakespeare, guide with the Cambridge Haunts: Harvard Square Ghost Tour, is like taking a steam punk–style time machine to the turn-of-the-century days of Harvard Yard. According to Shakespeare, Cambridge is oozing with the ghosts of the city's past.

"Most of the spirits on the tour enjoy us being there and telling their stories," mused Shakespeare. "It's almost as if we awakened a part of

Ashley Shakespeare, a ghost tour guide with Cambridge Haunts, had several close encounters with the ghosts from Cambridge's dark past while leading groups to site-specific haunts throughout Harvard Yard and Winthrop Park. *Photo by Ryan Miner.*

history that's been locked up for so long and these stories are finally being shared."

However, there's one Edwardian-era dandy spirit reportedly hanging outside Massachusetts Hall, the oldest building on Harvard's campus, who has made a guest appearance on Shakespeare's tour. His name? Holbrook Smith. "There's one spirit who doesn't care for me. I'm not sure it's just me or if he doesn't like us describing his appearance…Holbrook Smith 'had the saddest eyes I've ever seen.' He doesn't like that."

Ghosts with personalities? Shakespeare said his interaction with spirits is similar to his encounters with the living. "You become friends with people because you understand them or they entertain you for various reasons. I feel spirits do the same thing," he said. "They make themselves known to people because they want that fellowship. If you're a non-believer, I feel that spirits might make themselves known because they want you to believe."

Shakespeare, who helped spearhead the tour in 2012 based on the preliminary research from *Ghosts of Cambridge*, said he's been sensitive to the paranormal world most of his life. He was raised in Manhattan and spent his formative years in two highly active cities, New Orleans and Provincetown, before moving to Revere. "Growing up, I always felt like I was surrounded by a certain energy that I couldn't explain and I knew most people couldn't or wouldn't understand it. I spent a lot of time alone as a child. I was very shy and wasn't involved in a lot of activities boys my age were. I often felt misunderstood, and I feel that the spirits that surrounded me felt the same way," Shakespeare remembered. "It hasn't changed much in my adult life except I'm more in tune with and have found a certain way to communicate with some spirits that want to make themselves known to me," he continued.

As far as communicating with the spirit realm, Shakespeare said he usually has a physical reaction when a ghost is nearby. "I get chills and goose bumps," he explained. "Every hair on my body stands up. I also have been physically touched by spirits and have seen them open doors, turn on TVs and play with my pets."

The Cambridge Haunts guide said a few of his tours were standouts, including the Sunday evening following Harvard Square's Oktoberfest in 2012. Apparently, the Yard was teeming with spirits that night, and one guest captured a clear photo of what looked like a Civil War–era soldier peeking out of the structure's Annenberg Hall. "He's by far my favorite. I feel like we understand each other. He wants people to know who he is," Shakespeare said, adding that he's seen a full-bodied apparition of the Memorial Hall spirit peek outside the door leading to the hall's Memorial Transept.

"What I feel he has told me is that he was one of the students from Harvard who fought in the Civil War and ended up being killed in battle never being able to return and finish his education. He wanted to leave a legacy, but his life was taken away abruptly. He had dreams and ambitions, and he's thrilled that now through the tour we have given him a voice and a legacy."

Shakespeare's theory as to why the ghosts of Harvard Square were out and about during Oktoberfest? "They want to partake in the fun as well," he continued. "Harvard Square is bustling with entertainment, people having fun and enjoying themselves. The spirits don't want to be left out."

As far as other ghost tours with guides wearing over-the-top costumes popping up in Harvard Square, Shakespeare said it's obvious when a story is made up for pure entertainment value. "They drop the ball when it comes to history. In fact, I know that there are tours that just make up stories," he said. "They're fine if you just want to be entertained, but if you want stories based on actual history, Cambridge Haunts stands out."

In the ghost-tour circuit, Shakespeare said not all guides are legit. "If a tour guide doesn't believe in ghosts, they're almost robbing guests of the full experience," he added. "If a guide believes and can feel the spirit world, they have so much more to offer guests on their tour."

Shakespeare, who made a cameo in *Ghosts of Boston: Haunts of the Hub* in the write-up on Jacques Cabaret, an allegedly haunted drag-show venue in Boston's Bay Village, said there's a distinct difference in the ghosts he's encountered on the other side of the Charles River. "When I walk around Boston and feel spirit energy, it's often heavy, sad and sometimes angry," he emoted. "I have felt the presence of death on occasion walking around Boston. In Cambridge, the spirit energy is almost jovial. I feel welcomed and embraced by the ghosts of Cambridge. It may be due to the fact that Cambridge has always been a historically open and progressive town, unlike the Puritans of Boston."

As far as haunted hot spots in Harvard Square, Shakespeare said the construction surrounding Memorial Hall unleashed some unexpected activity. He also said the "Apthorp House spirit energy flows like a waterfall" when the Adams House gates on Plympton Street are opened. "It's always a surprise when spirits show up in places that aren't usually active," he said. "Guests who were born and raised in Cambridge are usually surprised about the city's history on the tour."

So, what spooks Shakespeare? "The spirit world doesn't scare me," he said with a laugh. "Certain spirits may spook me from time to time, but I'm never scared. I've embraced the spirit world, and I feel once you embrace something, it doesn't scare you any longer."

CHAPTER 1

BRITISH HAUNTS

The British are coming? If you believe in ghosts, they've been in Cambridge for hundreds of years. In fact, many of the city's alleged haunts were built on the hard soil of early Puritan thought and burgeoning anti-British sentiment.

When Thomas Dudley, deputy governor of the Massachusetts Bay Company, was on the hunt for a "fit place for a fortified town" in September 1630, he took a boat from Boston and walked up a "rounded hill" and ended up in what is now Winthrop Square. According to legend, Dudley stuck his cane in the ground and announced, "This is the place." The Puritans built homes in what is now the Harvard Square area in 1631, and Newtowne, which was renamed Cambridge in 1638 after England's college town, was born.

Fast-forward a century or so, and a cluster of seven incredibly wealthy British Loyalists built lavish estates along Watertown Road, later named Brattle Street. Known as Tory Row, these palatial houses were seized by the Continental army in 1775 and used as makeshift quarters and blood-splattered hospitals for the thousands of Patriots fighting for their independence. General George Washington, who assumed his role as the leader of the troops on July 3, 1775, set up headquarters at what is now the Longfellow House, located at 105 Brattle Street.

Many of the ghosts of Cambridge have ties to the historically significant estates dotting the streets of Tory Row. For example, the house known as Elmwood was built in 1767 by Thomas Oliver, the British-appointed

The Puritans built homes in what is now Harvard Square (originally named Newtowne) and renamed it Cambridge in 1638 after England's college town. The city's historic milestone, built in 1734 to mark the path of the Upper Boston Post Road, currently resides in Cambridge's Old Burial Ground. *Courtesy of the Library of Congress.*

lieutenant governor of Massachusetts. He assumed the position in early 1774, clearly a not-so-stellar time to be a Loyalist. On September 2, 1774, a mob of four thousand angry citizens surrounded Oliver's house located at 33 Elmwood Avenue. The gun-toting protesters forced Oliver to sign a letter of resignation, and he then fled to Boston and eventually England in 1776. Elmwood was seized by the Patriots and used as a hospital during the siege of Boston. The early seeds of anti-Loyalist protest were planted in Cambridge.

With the Revolutionary War–era bloodshed and strife serving as a spooky backdrop, Tory Row became the epicenter of sorts for the eighteenth-century spiritual movement based on the work of Emanuel Swedenborg, author of the book on the afterlife called *Heaven and Hell.* Poet James Russell Lowell, born on February 22, 1818, at Elmwood, became a diehard Swedenborg follower and would openly speak with his Tory Row neighbors, including Henry Wadsworth Longfellow's second wife, Frances, about his belief in spirits. According to Longfellow, Lowell "talked in a very Swedenborgian way of spiritual sympathies," wrote Martin Duberman in *James Russell Lowell.* "He has been long in the habit of seeing spirits and will not consider it a disease but a very natural phenomenon." Apparently,

Built in 1767 by Loyalist Thomas Oliver, the Tory Row estate known as Elmwood was seized by a mob of four thousand angry Patriots on September 2, 1774. Currently the private residence for Harvard's president, the Brattle Street haunt was also home to poet James Russell Lowell, known for his Victorian-era séances. *Courtesy of the Library of Congress.*

Lowell was frequently visited by his dead wife, Maria White, a women's rights activist and poet. She passed in 1853, at the age of thirty-two, and Lowell reportedly had "a distinct vision one bright afternoon in his easy chair of Maria White's face."

Elmwood, like many of the British-built estates on Brattle Street, boasts a bevy of tales from the crypt. Why? The late Jim McCabe, a noted ghost lore expert, believed the historic homes of Tory Row are ghost magnets. "The old Yankees may have been strange in some ways, but they kept the old buildings, which has made it attractive to many visitors—even ghosts," McCabe told the *Globe*. "Spirits are attracted to places they lived in. I think what attracts ghosts up here is that you don't tear down the buildings." Obviously, it should come as no surprise that one of the nation's oldest cities brims with spirits of those who lived and died during its hundreds of years of tumultuous history.

APTHORP HOUSE

Built in 1760, the clapboard Apthorp House—which predates the rest of Harvard's houses by several decades—is the main residence of Harvard's Adams House master, or a senior faculty member who presides over the upper-class dormitory. According to campus ghost lore, it's also home to the ghosts of Revolutionary War soldiers, among them British general John Burgoyne, who was imprisoned there during the war. Legend has it that Burgoyne's ghost still haunts the structure.

Apthorp House was one of the largest and most distinguished colonial residences in early Cambridge, surrounded by grounds that originally extended toward the Charles River. President and Harvard alum John Adams wrote that "a great house, at that time thought to be a splendid palace, was built by Mr. Apthorp at Cambridge." Its grandeur aroused suspicions among Cambridge's gossip mongers, who claimed that Christ Church's Reverend East Apthorp harbored a secret passion to become a bishop. The son of a British-born merchant, Apthorp fled to Britain in 1764 to avoid ridicule from the city's venom-spewing Congregationalists, who labeled his home "the Bishop's Palace."

After Apthorp escaped, John Borland purchased the house and added a third floor. However, his Tory leanings didn't sit well with the anti-Loyalist movement in the days leading up to the Revolutionary War in Cambridge,

Labeled the "Bishop's Palace," Apthorp House is the main residence of Harvard's Adams House masters and is allegedly haunted by the spirit of British general John Burgoyne, who was held prisoner in the estate after his surrender at the Battle of Saratoga in 1777. *Photo by Ryan Miner.*

and he left the house in 1775. Burgoyne, who retreated with troops after losing the Battle of Saratoga in 1777, was held prisoner in the estate. However, he had to pay rent.

Apparently, his dislike of his less-than-stellar living arrangements carried over to the afterlife. "Legend has it that Burgoyne's ghost still haunts the house," confirmed the Adams House website. "Like many subsequent tenants in Cambridge, he complained bitterly about the lack of furnishings and the exorbitant rent he was forced to pay."

Harvard's *Crimson* newspaper, whose office is located directly across the street from Apthorp, alluded to the "fearsome phantoms" lurking in the 250-year-old house. "I hear them rumbling about all the time," said Hannah L. Bouldin, who lived in the attic in the 1980s and claimed that Apthorp's soldier spirits helped her finish her exam. Jana M. Kiely, a former co-master at Adams, added fire to the Burgoyne myth. "General Burgoyne is still complaining about the high rent of Harvard property and wants the university to do something about it," Kiely mused.

Matthew Swayne, author of *America's Haunted Universities*, suggested that Burgoyne's ghost is possibly a residual apparition. "Burgoyne's anger and frustration must have imprinted itself on the psychic fiber of Apthorp," he wrote.

Apthorp House, which is surrounded by three "Gold Coast" dormitories that were built around 1900 to offer luxury accommodations for Harvard's elite, is literally in the center of what is possibly the college's most haunted corridor. "One house in particular—Adams House—is rumored to have the most ghosts," claimed Swayne in his book. Franklin D. Roosevelt, who lived in Westmorly Court (now B-17) from 1900 to 1904, was a famous Adams House alum. Oddly, there's a mysterious death associated with Roosevelt's distant relative Stewart Douglas Robinson, who tragically fell from his room at Hampden Hall, which is currently home to the Harvard Book Store.

To add some "boo" to the house's ghost lore, a novel written in 2000 by alum Sean Desmond called *Adams Fall* talked about the dorm's "severe Gothic quality." In fact, the murder mystery used the house as a metaphor for the protagonist's mental demise and described, in detail, the spook factor surrounding the "stone monster" structure. "A resident of Adams house's reportedly haunted B-entry, he's familiar with tales of phantom footsteps, vanished laundry, lurking shadows," Desmond wrote. "But when he begins to find himself the object of the house's cruel attentions, his world quickly begins to unravel." In one scene, Desmond's protagonist asked if Adams's B-entry was, in fact, haunted. "I know it is," responded a fictional female student. "It feels damned…The pipes make these weird noises. And sometimes there's the smell in the hallway and closets."

Oddly, there's a cryptic message circulating online alluding to the spirits of Adams House. "There's a ghost who lives underneath the dining hall in a crawl space," wrote an anonymous source. "If you have a tutor let you into the steam vents, you can hear her cry."

File under: haunted house

Hooper–Lee–Nichols House

If these walls could talk. Built in 1685 by Dr. Richard Hooper as a typical "first-period" farmhouse, the Hooper-Lee-Nichols House has seen its share of tragedy. "Some very grim things happened here," said Gavin W. Kleespies, executive director of the Cambridge Historical Society. "All of these houses on Tory Row are extremely old, and very bad things happened in all of them. As far as this house, it's pushing 330 years, and lots of people have died here," he said, giving a spirited tour of the second-oldest house in Cambridge. "Is it haunted? I don't know."

Kleespies, whose office is based in the historic Tory Row home, has an encyclopedic knowledge of the structure's tumultuous history. As far as ghost lore, however, he's quick to shoot down a rumor that has snowballed since the 1980s. According to the *Harvard Crimson*, "The Hooper-Lee-Nichols House on Brattle Street is said to be home to the ghosts of five Hessian mercenaries who fought in the Revolution. Legend has it they first appeared in 1915, when a library was built on the site of their graves. The Hessian quintet has been playing cards in the room ever since."

Fact? Kleespies said the Hessian legend is probably not historically accurate. "There's not a lot of truth to that story," he remarked. "There have been excavations to this site, and there are all sorts of myths that have been debunked. For example, people said that the house was a stop on the Underground Railroad. However, there's no evidence to support that claim."

The historian did point out a three-year period, from 1774 to 1777, when the house was vacated by noted British Loyalist judge Joseph Lee, who fled

The Hooper-Lee-Nichols House, located at 159 Brattle Street, was built in 1685 by Dr. Richard Hooper and was rumored to be home to the ghosts of five Hessian mercenaries who fought in the Revolution. Not true, according to the director of the Cambridge Historical Society. However, Gavin W. Kleespies said it's possible that its archives may be enchanted. *Photo by Ryan Miner.*

Tory Row days after the Powder Alarm, a precursor to the Revolution, when thousands of angry Patriots from surrounding towns prepared to march toward Boston for battle. However, Lee got out before the tumult. It seems that the September 1, 1774 alarm was a bit premature.

"Lee actually moved back in 1777 to reclaim his property, and unlike many of the houses in the area that were turned into quarters for the Convention Troops, his house was spared," Kleespies said, adding that it's unlikely that the German mercenaries, known as Hessians, were buried on the property. However, Kleespies said there's no concrete proof to contradict the claim. "It's possible because there were many officers who needed places to stay. But it was never recorded that Hessian soldiers actually stayed here," he said. "I mean, they could have stayed somewhere on Joseph Lee's property, but it's highly unlikely. The property was forty-five acres at the time, so it's inevitable that soldiers camped out somewhere near the house."

While Kleespies is quick to debunk the Hessian soldier myth, he does point out the macabre periods in the house's early years, especially after its original owner, Dr. Richard Hooper, died in 1691. "As far as the house being haunted, the American Revolution may be flashy, but the original owners have a very dark story," Kleespies continued. Hooper's wife, Elizabeth, took in boarders, and the property then began to fall into disrepair until her mysterious death in 1701.

"When Hooper died, he left a formidable estate. Within one year of his death, Hooper's wife fell on bad times and petitioned to be able to serve liquor. This is the 1690s, and by the time she passes, this house is just devastated. It's completely trashed," Kleespies said, adding that her dead body was found wrapped in a sheet. "There's a whole mystery about the house from 1701 to 1716. We don't know what happened. Are there any ghosts in the house from that period? Not sure. I wouldn't say that it was a house of ill repute, but it was definitely a house no one wanted to be associated with for fifteen years."

Fast-forward to the mid-nineteenth century, when the Nichols family moved into the Brattle Street estate. In 1850, George and Susan Nichols rented and began to renovate the house, installing a roof balustrade that was once part of Boston's St. Paul's Cathedral. One of the Nichols children married a Civil War officer, and her young daughter died tragically in the house. "It was the Fourth of July, and her daughter stepped on fireworks, got an infection and died," Kleespies said. "The Nichols daughter was devastated."

As far as residual energy lingering in the Hooper-Lee-Nichols House, Kleespies said he was convinced for years that the seventeenth-century structure was indeed haunted. In fact, Kleespies said he had a few close encounters in the early '90s. "I don't know if it was because I was a lot younger and impressionable, but if you asked me back then I would have said, without hesitation, that this place is definitely haunted," he said. "Creepy stuff happened. Doors opened and closed. Objects would mysteriously move to different locations. If you were here by yourself, you would hear noises."

Kleespies, who moved to Chicago to work on his master's, returned to the Hooper-Lee-Nichols House in 2008. Since his return, he hasn't encountered anything supernatural. "I'm here all the time—I'm even here Halloween at night—and nothing seems to bother me. Maybe the house is happier? It's hard to say."

However, the Hooper-Lee-Nichols's resident fellows, who sleep near the Cambridge Historical Society's archive, have approached Kleespies with creepy tales involving ghostly encounters. Kleespies's theory? Perhaps the spirits are attracted to the library's archives.

"One of our resident fellows would swear to this day that this house is haunted," Kleespies added. "Maybe it's the archives that's haunted? I don't know. We have a lot of stuff that meant a lot to many people who are no longer with us, like locks of hair, and if this place is haunted, it would be the archives. Maybe that's what's so scary."

File under: Tory woe

LONGFELLOW HOUSE

Henry Wadsworth Longfellow, the American literary icon and professor famous for his rhythmic cadences in poems like "Paul Revere's Ride" and "The Village Blacksmith," moved to Cambridge in 1854 and set up home in the so-called haunted house where he both lived and died. Longfellow set up shop at the mid-Georgian mansion, known as the Vassall-Craigie-Longfellow House, which was built in 1759 by Major John Vassall, a wealthy Tory Row Loyalist.

Before Longfellow, George Washington lived there for ten months between July 1775 and April 1776 and used the building as his headquarters when he was leading the newly formed Continental army. For the record,

Built in 1759 by Major John Vassall, the historic Longfellow House on Tory Row briefly served as George Washington's headquarters in July 1775 and later became iconic poet Henry Wadsworth Longfellow's estate. Visitors who tour the house claim to see the spirit of a lady in white, believed to be Longfellow's wife, Frances "Fanny" Appleton, who was tragically burned to death there in 1861. *Photo by Ryan Miner.*

Washington planned the Siege of Boston from the Tory Row house, and according to Hugh Howard's *Houses of the Founding Fathers*, Washington found the stellar view of the Charles River particularly useful. His maneuvering resulted in the evacuation of 120 ships carrying thousands of British soldiers and Loyalists back to England.

It's that view that initially attracted Longfellow to the historic Brattle Street estate. Elizabeth Craigie owned the house in the early 1800s and rented rooms out to Harvard students. Longfellow became one of Craigie's lodgers in 1837 and had a close encounter with what he believed was a full-bodied apparition of America's founding father. In April 1840, Longfellow watched the gardener's house in the back catch fire and burn down. Locals gathered to put out the blaze, and Longfellow shuddered in awe as he noticed something odd emerge from the smoke. "In the midst of it all, I saw slowly riding under the elms on the green in front of the house, a figure on horseback," he wrote in a letter. "It seemed like the ghost of Washington, directing the battle."

Longfellow's first wife, Mary Potter, died in 1835 following a miscarriage. He soon began courting Frances "Fanny" Appleton, the daughter of a wealthy Boston industrialist. He would walk over the Boston Bridge from Cambridge to the Appletons' home in Beacon Hill. In 1906, the bridge was renamed the Longfellow Bridge in honor of the late great poet.

After seven years of courting and dealing with "periods of neurotic depression," Longfellow received a letter from Appleton that would temporarily quell his anxiety. On May 10, 1843, Appleton agreed to marry Longfellow, and as a wedding gift from his wife's father, the two moved into the historic Vassall-Craigie House. Longfellow fathered six children with Appleton.

According to lore, their Tory Row estate was teeming with spirits. "The story that this house is haunted has been current for several generations," wrote Dorothy Dudley in *Theatrum Majorum* in 1875. Longfellow, skeptical of the ghost lore, would muse about an encounter he had coming home one night from the Dante Club. "When he crossed the garden he was startled by a white figure swaying before him," remembered William Dean Howells in *The White Mr. Longfellow*. "But he knew that the only way was to advance upon it. He pushed boldly forward, and was suddenly caught under the throat—by the clothesline—with a long nightgown on it." In other words, Longfellow had a logical explanation to debunk all the conjecture surrounding the spirits inhabiting his house.

It was all hocus pocus. Or was it?

His wife, however, was more of a believer. In fact, Fanny's brother Tom Appleton was interested in the Spiritualism movement and introduced a well-known intuitive, Alice Goodrich, to the Longfellows. Goodrich, whom Appleton described as a "very strong medium," would allegedly channel the spirits and write cryptic messages from the dead, known as "automatic writing," that could be deciphered when held up to a mirror. Goodrich wrote one of her spirit letters to Longfellow, a benevolent message that ends with "let us drink."

Unfortunately, Goodrich's so-called psychic abilities couldn't predict the horrors Longfellow would experience at home. On July 9, 1861, his wife was in the library reportedly sealing locks of their children's hair with a lit candle and envelopes. Somehow the wax—or, as in one theory suggested by their daughter, Allegra, a lit match—caught her summer dress on fire, and it was quickly engulfed in flames. Longfellow was taking a nap and rushed in to throw a rug around his wife, but it was too late to save her. Appleton became what was described as a human torch and, in essence,

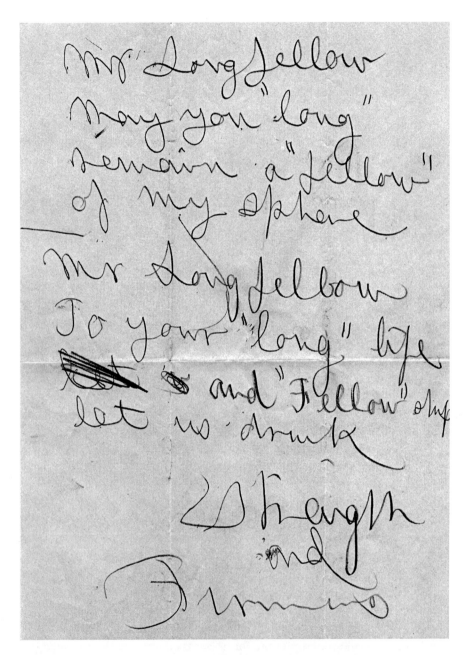

The Longfellows were visited by Alice Goodrich, a well-known medium who would allegedly channel the spirits and write cryptic messages from the dead, known as "automatic writing." The handwritten letter ends with "let us drink." *Courtesy National Park Service, Longfellow House–Washington's Headquarters National Historic Site.*

burned alive. She died the following morning at 10:00 a.m. after requesting a cup of coffee in her room.

The poet was injured by the blaze and unable to attend her funeral. According to reports, he grew his trademark beard to cover up the scars from the tragedy. However, his emotional scars continued to linger. "Everywhere he walked in the house, he told me later, he saw mother," wrote E. Ashley Rooney in *Cambridge, Massachusetts: Ghosts, Legends & Lore*, paraphrasing their daughter's diary. "She was in the library knitting, in the study talking and laughing with him, in the parlor dancing with us."

Coincidentally, her funeral was held on what would have been the couple's eighteenth wedding anniversary. "Frances was laid on a table in the center covered with flowers including white roses," wrote Rob Velella in his *Haunted Houses* tour. "She also had a wreath of orange blossoms around her head."

After his wife's death, Longfellow was tormented by the real-life horror he had witnessed in the library. According to his daughter's recollections, as told to Rooney, he had late-night conversations with the ghost of his dead wife and would dance with her apparition. "I think that ultimately he believed that she was there and because he believed, we believed," Rooney wrote. "Her spirit hovered over us."

Longfellow turned to laudanum and ether to self-medicate and begged "not to be sent to an asylum." The poet, who took a break from writing, said he was "inwardly bleeding to death." His heart was broken.

On September 21, 1865, Longfellow was mysteriously visited by one of the Fox sisters, major players in the Spiritualism movement, who allegedly interacted with the spirit world in the form of mysterious rapping sounds, or what Longfellow called "spiritual manifestations." The grieving poet invited Kate Fox into the library, the scene of his wife's death, and he heard a series of phantom rappings, which included "knocks on the door, on the table, on the floor," he recalled in a letter.

Longfellow died in 1882 and was buried next to his wife in Mount Auburn Cemetery.

So is the Longfellow House haunted? People who have toured the mansion have seen a lady in white, wearing period costume, in the bedroom upstairs. Laura West, an intuitive at Divine Lotus Healing, said she's heard of people being "touched in specific spots in the house," she wrote online. She also learned about the lady in white from the Longfellow House guide. "Once or twice, she's heard other tour guides tell stories about people on the tours, asking 'who was that actress upstairs sitting on

Henry Wadsworth Longfellow, grieving the tragic loss of his wife, was mysteriously visited by Kate Fox—one of the sisters who claimed to connect with spirits through phantom rappings—and heard the eerie knockings in the library where his late wife was fatally burned. The poet passed in 1882 and is memorialized in Longfellow Park by a bronze statue designed by Daniel Chester French in 1913. *Photo by Ryan Miner.*

the bed? Her clothing looked so authentic.' Only to discover that the staff doesn't employ actors in period costume."

Longfellow's own poem "Haunted Houses" oddly answers the is-it-or-isn't-it question: "All houses wherein men have lived and died are haunted houses," he wrote. "Through the open doors the harmless phantoms on their errands glide with feet that make no sound upon the floors."

File under: ghost writer

CHAPTER 2
COLONIAL HAUNTS

C ambridge became an unlikely hot spot in the days leading up to the Revolutionary War. However, there was little indication of this overnight upheaval in the early 1700s. Its Sleepy Hollow–esque vibe, modeled after the picturesque English villages its Puritan founders had left behind, turned into tumult as nine thousand citizen soldiers from rustic country towns scattered throughout New England gathered in the Cambridge Common in 1775. Before the "shot heard 'round the world" in Concord on April 29, Cambridge boasted about two thousand residents, 90 percent of whom were descendants of the seven hundred Puritans who had sailed from England to Newtowne in 1630.

According to legend, General George Washington assumed his role as commander of the thousands of militiamen known as the Continental army beneath an elm tree in the Common. This epic scene, which has been immortalized by illustrators and storytellers over the years, is believed to be more myth than fact. According to Richard Ketchum's *The World of George Washington*, the emerging leader was concerned with his crew of untrained militiamen, calling them a "mixed multitude of people…under very little discipline, order or government."

In other words, Washington had his work cut out for him.

The sudden upheaval in 1775 is believed to be the source of some of the residual energy that left a psychic imprint of sorts on the weathered streets and centuries-old buildings in Harvard Square. According to master psychic Denise Fix, a handful of Cambridge's ghosts can be traced back to the

General George Washington assumed his role as commander of the thousands of militiamen known as the Continental army beneath an elm tree in the Cambridge Common. While the epic story involving the tree has been debunked by historians, psychics claim a handful of Cambridge's ghosts can be traced back to the Revolutionary War. *Courtesy of the Boston Public Library, Print Department.*

Revolutionary War. "Some of the spirits around us are wearing uniforms," said Fix during a visit to Cambridge's Old Burying Ground. "There's a lot of residual energy associated with men from George Washington's era. I keep seeing men wearing [tricorn] hats."

The precursor to the American Revolutionary War, known as the Battle of Lexington and Concord, in April 1775 claimed the lives of six Cantabrigians. Oddly, they weren't killed during the battle but during the British retreat. Two locals, Jabez Wyman and Jason Winship, were downing a few ales at Cooper's Tavern, which is located near Beech Street in North Cambridge. "The King's regular troops under the command of General [Thomas] Gage, upon their return from blood and slaughter, which they had made at Lexington and Concord, fired more than one hundred bullets into the house where we dwell, through doors and windows," recalled Rachel Cooper, who ran the tavern with her husband, Benjamin, in an interview one month after the horrific incident. "The two aged gentlemen were immediately most barbarously and inhumanly murdered by them, being stabbed through in many places, their heads mangled, skulls broke and their brains out on the floor and walls of the house."

Both Wyman and Winship were buried in Cambridge's Old Burying Ground in Harvard Square.

John Hicks, a diehard Patriot who trekked eight miles to participate in the Boston Tea Party, also died in April 1775 as the British marched in full retreat toward Boston. Trying to launch a surprise attack against the redcoats, Hicks hid behind some barrels at Watson's Corner in North Cambridge. He was joined by Moses Richardson and Isaac Gardner, the first Harvard graduate (class of 1747) who died for liberty. They all were bayoneted by the redcoats, and Hicks was shot through the heart. Williams Marcy, who thought he was seeing a parade, was shot as he sat on a wall and cheered.

"Hicks, Richardson and Marcy were buried in an unmarked grave and were soon forgotten as Cambridge became an armed camp of several thousand minutemen gathered from all over New England to oppose

John Hicks, a diehard Patriot who participated in the Boston Tea Party, was savagely murdered by British troops while trying to launch a surprise attack at Watson's Corner in North Cambridge. His house, located across from Winthrop Park in Harvard Square, is currently home to Harvard's Kirkland House library. *Photo by Ryan Miner.*

the British," reported the Cambridge Historical Commission. "In 1875, the Patriot's common grave was found in the Old Burying Ground and monuments were erected there and in front of the Watson house at 2154 Massachusetts Ave." Today, there's a concrete marker commemorating what was Cambridge's version of the Boston Massacre.

Hicks, who was among the casualties from the era, lived in what is currently Harvard's Kirkland House library. Israel Putnam—who spearheaded the Battle of Bunker Hill and is arguably one of the more colorful officers of the Revolution, thanks to folklore from his youth that suggested he killed the last wolf in Connecticut—moved into the Hicks house, which was built in 1762 and is located across from Winthrop Park in Harvard Square.

Are the ghosts of Cambridge's Revolutionary War past still hanging out in the area? It's possible. Paranormal investigators like Adam Berry from *Ghost Hunters* believe that residual energy associated with this tumultuous time in American history may have left a supernatural imprint. "Anytime there's a traumatic event, it could be left behind," Berry said. "If you walk into a room and two people have been arguing, fiercely, you can feel that weirdness that they've created or energy they emit spewing at each other. I do think there's a form of energy that can be left behind from a traumatic event or any kind of murder or suicide in a room. The theory is that maybe that energy goes into the walls and lingers there."

OLD BURYING GROUND

When it comes to the ghosts of Cambridge's past, all paths lead to the corner of Massachusetts Avenue and Garden Street. Known as "God's Acre," the Old Burying Ground was established before 1635 and preceded both Christ Church and First Parish. Harvard presidents and paupers were buried there. Paranormal investigators, like Adam Berry from Syfy's *Ghost Hunters*, believe the older the cemetery, the more intimidating. "Cemeteries are where they go to rest and don't want to be bothered," Berry told the author. "I don't believe they're bound or held captive in that specific spot. However, I do feel they're abundant."

The city of Cambridge was known as Newtowne until 1638, and the town's oldest cemetery was rumored to be around Brattle and Ash Streets. It's long gone. "It was deemed that the cemetery was not safe from the intrusion of wild animals, and the cemetery was not used after 1634," wrote

The only burial ground in Cambridge for two hundred years, the Old Burying Ground boasts a cross-section of the city's population ranging from Harvard presidents to Revolutionary War–era soldiers. It's also home to spirits that reportedly visit the cemetery and are supposedly itching to make contact with the living. *Courtesy of the Library of Congress.*

Roxie Zwicker in *Massachusetts Book of the Dead.* "There is no indication of where the cemetery is in the city today, as it has been lost to time and urban development."

As the only burial spot for nearly two hundred years, the Old Burying Ground received a cross section of the population, including slaves Neptune Frost and Cato Stedman and at least nineteen Revolutionary War soldiers. Burial spaces in the early years weren't permanently marked, and the cemetery contains many more remains than are in the 1,218 known graves. Most of the monuments are slate headstones, and some markers, including those crafted by Joseph Lamson from Charlestown, portray "evil demons of death" with imps carrying coffins away. The oldest gravestone, dated 1653, belongs to Anne Erinton, but the stone may have been placed later, as headstones didn't come into general use until the 1670s. Excluding the tombs, the cemetery's last known burial was in 1811.

There's also a subterranean tunnel. As in Britain, upper-class families wished to be interred in burial vaults rather than in caskets placed directly

Penelope Vassall, a Loyalist who fled her Tory Row estate in the days leading up to the Revolutionary War, spent her last days in Antigua and struggled financially before making a postmortem return to her beloved Cambridge. Vassall is interred in the family's subterranean tomb beneath Christ Church. *Photo by Ryan Miner.*

in the ground. The John Vassall tomb is the most elaborate. Last opened in 1862, it contained twenty-five caskets, including that of Andrew Craigie, who acquired the family's Christ Church pew and burial plot along with the Vassall estate in 1792.

Mythology surrounding the Vassall family continues to polarize historians. Penelope Vassall, who fled Cambridge during the Revolutionary War, supposedly paid twenty pounds in 1722 to free the child of her driver Tony from slavery. "Cambridge, becoming a military camp, was neither a pleasant nor safe residence for those who still adhered to King George, so Madame Vassall departed in haste to Antigua," wrote Dorothy Dudley in *Theatrum Majorum*. "Popular tradition asserts that the slaves of the Vassalls were inhumanely treated. There seems to be no foundation of this report." Penelope Vassall visited Cambridge after the Revolution and, after struggling financially, was buried in the subterranean vault beneath Christ Church. She was joined by Tony's son Darby Vassall, an African American man, who was eventually freed from slavery. He was the last person to be interred in the tomb on October 15, 1861. Leave it to Cambridge to challenge the status quo.

The Old Burying Ground also boasts Harvard's first president, Henry Dunster, who was banished from Cambridge for challenging the Puritans' views on baptism. In 1654, he begged church authorities to allow his family to stay in the modest home he had built with his own money, but he was forced to move to Plymouth County and was replaced by Charles Chauncy, a local minister who believed in the faith-based tradition. Dunster's unorthodox views earned him an unsavory "Harvard heretic" moniker because he interrupted church services and declined to have his fourth child baptized. Puritan elders believed the Devil was working through the Harvard president, and after meeting with magistrates in Boston, he was forced to resign. The university's founding president, who lived the last five years of his life in Scituate, died a broken man in 1659. Dunster's last wish? He wanted to be buried in Cambridge, close to his beloved Harvard.

But is the Old Burying Ground haunted? Perhaps. Curiosity seekers on the Cambridge Haunts ghost tour have snapped tons of photos with so-called orbs, and a few swear they've seen what looked like a full-bodied apparition. Master psychic Denise Fix, who visited the cemetery with the author, made contact with Seth Hastings, who passed on October 15, 1775. Fix said the "gentleman whose benevolence extended to all," as indicated by his gravestone, was itching to make contact with the living. According to Fix, Hastings was a cordial man with a sense of humor even though he's six feet under.

Berry, who spent hours in old cemeteries armed with an EVP recorder before auditioning for *Ghost Hunters Academy* and then officially joining TAPS (The Atlantic Paranormal Society) team, said burial grounds attract spirits. "Cemeteries have a lot of activity. The [spirits] want to talk to you, and they may have a story to pass on," he remarked. "As investigators, we try not to go on feelings, because you can't prove feelings. But you can't ignore your biggest organ, which is your skin and the goose bumps that you get, and feeling like you're being watched."

File under: grave encounters

PROSPECT HILL

The creepy castle atop Somerville's historic Prospect Hill oozes a something-wicked-this-way-comes vibe. Built in 1902 to commemorate the hill's role as a Revolutionary and Civil War fortification, the castle boasts killer views of the Boston skyline. It was its bird's-eye location that initially attracted George Washington, then the Continental army's commander in chief, to the site as he hashed out plans for the Siege of Boston. "From the summit of the hill, an extensive view of the surrounding country could be obtained, thus affording an excellent opportunity to note movements of the opposing forces. Immediate preparations were made to erect fortifications, beginning at a point near Union Square and extending over the hill," wrote Albert Haskell in his *Historical Guidebook of Somerville*. "After the battle of Bunker Hill the Americans withdrew to this hill, taking shelter behind the earthworks."

Historians claim that Washington raised an early version of the American flag, called the Grand Union Flag, on January 1, 1776. However, it's up for debate whether this momentous event—which was reportedly greeted with cheers and a thirteen-gun salute—was in fact the country's first flag raising. We do know that the initial flag was transferred to a fort in the Boston Harbor after the British retreated.

In addition to its glory days as a pre–Revolutionary War fortification, the so-called citadel has a dark history as a makeshift prison for British general

Somerville's Prospect Hill, known as the spot where George Washington raised an early version of the American flag on January 1, 1776, has a little-known history as a makeshift prison for Revolution-era British and Hessian soldiers. Apparently, conditions were miserable. The hot spot has been investigated by the team from *Paranormal Hood* and is potentially haunted. *Courtesy of the Boston Public Library, Print Department.*

John Burgoyne's Hessian troops, hired German mercenaries shipped over to Boston and used as guns for hire. Apparently, it was a tough winter for the prisoners of war, who had a helluva time finding wood for heat. "The British and Hessian soldiers, while in Somerville, were quartered in the old barracks left by the Americans after the Siege of Boston," wrote Charles Darwin Elliot in *Somerville's History*. "The wind whistled through the thin walls, the rain came through the roofs, the snow lay in drifts on the floor," complained one prisoner of war cited in Elliot's book.

General Friedrich Adolf Riedesel, Burgoyne's wing man and general of the German troops, echoed the complaints. "Indeed the greater number of the soldiers are so miserably lodged that they are unable to shelter themselves from cold and rain in this severe season of the year," Riedesel noted in his diary. "The soldiers, of whom twenty to twenty-four occupy the same barrack, are without light at night. Three of them share a bed," he continued, adding that they were imprisoned in squalor for an entire year, beginning in winter 1777 to November 1778.

However, it's these "miserable" conditions that may have left a psychic imprint on the ominous castle sitting atop Prospect Hill. Joe "Jiggy" Webb, founder of the paranormal investigation team called HooDeez, checked out Prospect Hill in July 2012. "It's so eerie out there when it gets dark," Webb said, presenting the footage shot for his online *Paranormal Hood* TV show. "I've been on many investigations, and this one definitely spooked me," he says, referring to a scene where he's standing in front of the castle and he feels something touch him. "It could have been a bug, but something makes me jump. I felt like something grabbed me."

In the footage, there is a full moon poetically perched above the castle's infamous flagstaff.

During the investigation, Webb reached inside the castle's bars to grab the team's motion detector. Then it moved. "Something pulls it forward," he said. "I'm not touching it, and something is obviously moving it." In the video, it's clear that he reached for the device and then it flew off the concrete ledge.

Webb, who wanted to investigate locations that deviate from the norm— like the Lizzie Borden house in Fall River and the Omni Parker House in Boston—surveyed the area with a handheld Ghost Meter Pro. In the video, his ghost-hunting device is buzzing and flashing. And then the investigation got freaky. Webb and Marlon Orozco, a local videographer and *Paranormal Hood* producer, captured a distinct voice using what he called a spirit box (a contraption used to contact ghosts through radio frequencies).

When Webb asked if the spirit had a name, there's a clear response to the question: "Brian," the voice from beyond responded. Then Webb asked, "Do you want us to leave?" The spirit's response: "Not."

Webb isn't sure who, or what, his team captured in Prospect Hill. "He could be a soldier," Webb continued. "Brian is a common name and it's an old English name, so it could have been someone who was there during one of the wars."

File under: haunted hill

WADSWORTH HOUSE

Built in 1726, this Early Georgian building is one of the few large houses not constructed by a Tory. Facing Massachusetts Avenue and an architectural anomaly of sorts thanks to its five-bay façade and simplistic Colonial design, Wadsworth House served as the primary residence for the president of Harvard until 1849. Over the years, the house would host visiting ministers and student boarders (including Ralph Waldo Emerson). The second-oldest surviving structure on Harvard's campus, the house lost its front yard when Massachusetts Avenue was widened.

Wadsworth House was also a major player in the days leading up to the Revolutionary War. The fight for independence began on April 19, 1775, and thousands of armed men from all over New England gathered in Cambridge. However, there was a housing shortage. Soldiers camped in the Cambridge Common while Harvard, responding to the growing anti-Tory sentiment and concerned about student safety, canceled classes on May 1 and allowed displaced soldiers to set up temporary shelter in its buildings. Oddly, classes took a wartime field trip nearly twenty miles away in Concord when classes resumed on October 5.

On June 15, 1775, the Continental Congress appointed George Washington as commander in chief of the army, and he assumed his role as the leader of the troops on July 3, 1775. Washington set up his first headquarters at Wadsworth House, located at 1341 Massachusetts Avenue, and it's said that he hashed out plans to oust King George from Boston in the historic landmark's parlor room. Washington, who remained in Cambridge until April 1776, later moved into his primary residence located at the Longfellow House on Brattle Street. Apparently, Wadsworth was in complete disrepair at the time.

Harvard's Wadsworth House, built in 1726 and used as temporary headquarters for George Washington in the days leading up to the Revolutionary War, is rumored to sport a residual haunting of a "grim character in a tricorn hat and cloak," according to a cleaning lady vacuuming alone in the colonial-era structure. *Photo by the author.*

In addition to its role in the Revolutionary War, there are several reports of Washington-era residual hauntings that continue to linger in the chambers of the colonial haunt. "One account explains that early one morning, forty years ago, a cleaning lady vacuuming alone in Wadsworth House saw a grim character in a tricorn hat and cloak silently come down the stairs and go out the door," reports the *Crimson* in 1997. The reporter, however, never confirmed the rumor, adding that "none of the staff at the Wadsworth House have heard anything about a man in a tricorn hat."

An article dating back to 1986 confirmed a similar story. "Over at Wadsworth House, where Washington once slept, ghosts of American Patriots wearing tricorn hats and cloaks have not haunted the colonial building in at least 25 years," the *Crimson* added.

Spirits wearing tricorn hats? Yep, Harvard Square allegedly has them. For the record, a residual haunting isn't technically a ghost but a playback or recording of a past event. Based on the so-called Stone Tape theory, apparitions aren't intelligent spirits that interact with the living but psychic imprints that happen especially during moments of high tension, such as a murder or during intense moments of a person's life. According to the hypothesis, residual hauntings are simply non-interactive playbacks, similar to a movie.

While Wadsworth's residual haunting is clearly a Patriot, there's a similar story involving a British redcoat in the bowels of the Boylston T station, the oldest rapid transport platform in the United States. According to ghost tour Haunted Boston, there are reports of "a British soldier, in full redcoat regalia, standing in the middle of the tracks and holding a musket."

Trolley conductors usually see this gun-toting apparition during the early morning shift or the wee hours of the night. The ghostly trek from Arlington to Boylston is rumored to be a hazing ritual of sorts for new T recruits. They slam on their brakes, obviously freaked out by the human-shaped mist, while the more experienced drivers get a kick out of spooking the newcomers.

Why would a Revolution-era casualty of war haunt Boylston station? During the gruesome excavation project in 1895, historian Samuel A. Green was called in to identify the skeletal remains of what turned out to be a mass grave site. "It is impossible to tell who is buried there, but we know that the British during their eight months' occupancy of Boston in the revolutionary struggle, buried some of their soldiers who were killed at Bunker Hill there," he told the *Boston Daily Globe* in April 1895. "Others who died from the effects of wounds in this battle were also interred there."

The *Globe* reported that on the days the excavation took place, hordes of curious onlookers gathered around the dig site, prompting police to set up a barricade. A canvas had to be "spread over a couple of pieces of joint to shut off the view of the spectators in the vicinity of the tombs." Articles of hair and clothing were oddly well preserved within the subterranean pool of bodies, even though the battle occurred more than one hundred years before the dig. Some say many of the British soldiers were missing limbs and other body parts because of shoddy, pre-sterilization medical care. There's a generic gravestone at the Central Burying Ground honoring the desecrated

900 to 1,100 bodies uncovered during the trolley station excavation. The marker reads: "Here were re-interred the remains of persons found under the Boylston Street mall during the digging of the subway 1895."

Based on ghost lore, hauntings have been associated with the lack of proper burial or a later desecration of the grave. Countless spirits, according to paranormal researchers, have been traced to missing gravestones or vandalism of a resting place. In regards to the pre-Revolution spirit allegedly lingering in Wadworth House, it's likely that the residual haunting is a psychic imprint of sorts associated with the intense military strategy sessions in the summer of 1775.

In November 1973, the senior editor of *Harvard Magazine*, with offices formerly located in the Wadsworth House, wrote an article called "The House Is Haunted and We Like It That Way," referring to the tricorn hat–wearing spirits allegedly haunting the almost three-hundred-year-old landmark. "For a society of rationalists, Harvardians are surprisingly interested in the supernatural," mused *Harvard Magazine*'s editor in 1998. "Clearly, all this talk about ghosts concerns Harvard's continuity and history and traditions—not séances and the ectoplasm."

Seriously? Based on reports from the cleaning lady who spotted the "grim character in a tricorn hat and cloak" levitating down the stairs, perhaps the ghosts of Harvard are more than a personification of the Ivy League's storied past. It's possible that the spirits of Wadsworth House are, in fact, ghostly reminders of the historically significant military sessions spearheaded by Washington in 1775.

File under: residual reminders

CHAPTER 3

HARVARD HAUNTS

H istory and mystery lurk in just about every crimson corner at
Cambridge's prestigious Ivy League. Harvard University is full of
secrets, and its ghost lore reflects this centuries-old legacy of dead presidents
and long-gone intelligentsia. Spine-chilling tales of unexplained sounds,
phantom knocking and full-bodied apparitions have become a rite of
passage for the uninitiated, college-bound progeny adapting to life in one of
the Hogwarts-style halls scattered throughout Harvard Yard.

Elizabeth Tucker, a professor of English at Binghamton University and
author of *Haunted Halls: Ghostlore of American College Campuses*, said that
collegiate ghost stories are morality plays for the modern era. "They educate
freshmen about how to live well in college," she explained in a 2007 interview,
adding that the cautionary tales serve as spooky metaphors of fear, disorder
and insanity. They also reflect students' interest in their college's historical
legacy. Yep, campus ghost lore is a paranormal pep rally of sorts. "You don't
find ghost stories at schools without a sense of pride," Tucker continued.
"School spirits reflect school spirit."

The difference between Harvard's specters and other run-of-the-mill
ghosts haunting universities throughout the country? Their spirits are
wicked smart. Harvard's Massachusetts Hall has one respectable-looking
student who returns every fall claiming to be a member of the class of
1914. Apparently, the residual apparition of Holbrook Smith never got
the memo that he was kicked out of the Ivy League almost a century ago.
There's also a Civil War–era apparition that allegedly haunts Memorial

If school spirits reflect school spirit, Harvard is arguably the country's most historic and potentially most haunted university in the country. According to psychics, the ghosts of Harvard walk through the Yard, and many don't know that they've passed. *Courtesy Boston Public Library, Print Department.*

Hall. In 1929, a proctor reported seeing a man, who wasn't enrolled in the class, show up with a blue book in hand. The school spirit was known as the Memorial Hall ghost, and the "left behind" (a spirit that doesn't know he's dead) kept returning to class to finish the test—even though he died long ago.

Adam Berry, winner of Syfy's *Ghost Hunters Academy* and investigator with The Atlantic Paranormal Society (TAPS) on *Ghost Hunters*, said Harvard has the potential to be America's most haunted campus. "Because of the history, there are so many interesting places that could be investigated," he said. "It had tons of activity during the Revolutionary and Civil Wars. There must be spirits left behind, milling about and checking out the status of the community they built way back when."

MaryLee Trettenero, a Boston-based psychic intuitive known for her residual energy work spearheading the Spirits of Charlestown Ghost Project, suggested that Berry's hunch was correct. "I feel really heavy right now and I keep seeing graves, as if dead bodies are buried around here," she told the author during an impromptu walk-through near Widener Library. "I see people who are long gone walking [in the Yard], and many of them don't know they've passed."

In addition to Harvard's ghost lore, the university has secrets. However, not all of them are doom and gloom. For example, the iconic John Harvard statue positioned in front of the allegedly haunted University Hall is known as the bronze statue of three lies. The Puritan-dressed model for the statue was Sherman Hore, a member of the class of 1882. After establishing the college in 1636, Harvard died in 1638, long before the statue was sculpted. So it's not actually the college's namesake depicted in the piece.

Tourists flock to the monument and believe rubbing his shiny foot will bring them good luck, kind of like the pilgrims who travel to St. Peter's Basilica in Rome to touch the foot of St. Peter. The difference between Harvard and St. Peter's, however, is that Harvard students reportedly urinate on the very

Going to the John? The iconic John Harvard statue in front of the allegedly haunted University Hall is also known as the statue of three lies. Also, Harvard's shiny right foot has stoically born the brunt of a ghastly undergraduate tradition. *Courtesy of the Library of Congress.*

foot that tourists rub. Heard of going to the John, right? Probably not how the Charlestown-based minister would like to be remembered.

Like the subterranean steam tunnels that connect the university's buildings, Harvard's darker mysteries are buried in the hard soil of Puritan thought.

"In an institution with a past as long and as storied as Harvard's, one would expect at least a few ghost stories," wrote the *Crimson* in 1997. "Surprisingly, however, there is little on record."

Contrary to the report, the Yard is full of fearsome phantoms. They're just hiding. The ghosts of Harvard are lurking in the shadows, behind the historic buildings dotting the campus and waiting for their stories to be told. Every school has its secrets.

CABOT HOUSE

Radcliffe College, formerly an all-female liberal arts institution that joined forces with Harvard in 1967 and completely merged with the university in 1999, has ghost lore too. Its iconic Radcliffe Quadrangle, which boasts early twentieth-century dormitories—including Briggs Hall, which was built in the early 1920s and became part of the Cabot House cluster similar to the house structure in *Harry Potter*—sports a few tales from the crypt. In fact, one story centers on a well-respected Radcliffe alum who died suddenly of pneumonia at her home in South Hadley on March 14, 1923.

Her name? Margaret Coleman Waites. The professor of classics wasn't quite forty years old when she tragically passed. However, her legacy lives on in a collection of beloved books and antiques now housed in what is known as the Cabot Library Suite, a popular upper-class dormitory with five bedrooms and a killer common area. What was once the Cabot House library, chock-full of "funky old library book shelves and books," now hosts some serious parties and "seems to attract eclectic personalities and tastes," reported the *Crimson*.

It's also allegedly a hot spot for paranormal activity. "This room is haunted by Margaret Coleman Waites," insisted Matt O'Malley in 2003, pointing to a placard bearing her name above the fireplace. "I've definitely been visited by spirits in my sleep."

Nine Harvard guys decorated Waites's library, which is now co-ed, with tinfoil wallpaper coupled with blue-and-red construction paper accents. "The boys say that the classic dark wood bookshelves, which came complete with several volumes of Shakespeare, not to mention about 30 rotting CUE Guides [student evaluations of professors], add a touch of sophistication to their party scene," continued the article. "Haunted or not, the Library Suite tends to come with high expectations and a reputation for campus revelry."

Harvard's former all-female dormitory in the Radcliffe Quadrangle boasts a to-die-for library suite at Cabot House's Briggs Hall. Apparently, the spirit of a long-passed alum, Margaret Coleman Waites, haunts the room and is possibly attached to the books she bequeathed to Radcliffe. *Courtesy of Harvard University, Radcliffe Archives.*

Party scene? Waites, who was a serious scholar and professor of classics at Mount Holyoke College, specialized in Roman literature and archaeology. A few months after her death in 1923, her personal library was transferred to Briggs Hall. It contained Roman-inspired antiquities, including books and photographs. Libraries were important to Waites, as expressed by her Radcliffe peer and dear friend Professor Florence Gragg in a written eulogy. "Miss Waites was a productive scholar who allowed no excuse of pressure of class work or inadequacy of library facilities or ill-health to interfere with her research or her enjoyment of it," Gragg wrote in a bulletin from the Classical Association of New England. "She had indomitable pluck."

If the Cabot Library Suite is in fact haunted, it's possible that Waites's "indomitable pluck" is attached to the books she bequeathed to Radcliffe. According to paranormal researchers who believe in the Stone Tape theory, inanimate objects like books can absorb some form of energy from living beings and "recorded" during an intense moment of their lives. "A residual haunting—trapped energy—is more likely stored by an item near the event," explained the authors of *Haunted Objects: Stories of Ghosts on Your Shelf.* "It becomes almost like a character…a crystal lamp or a setting of silverware becomes haunted and then replays the moment when the right environmental tumblers fall into place. The object can be moved to another location and when the situation is right, the recording replays, creating a haunting."

Waites, who suffered during the last days of her life with pneumonia, died suddenly at the prime of her career. It's plausible that her beloved library absorbed her residual energy. She did love her books.

So, if O'Malley's assertion that he's been "visited by spirits" in his sleep is true, it's possible that Waites is making a postmortem plea, begging the party boys of Cabot to respect her belongings. Meanwhile, the library suite continues to be a popular late-night destination. Based on a recent YouTube video called "Cabot Cribs," Waites's legacy, which included a plaque honoring her life, has been covered up by a larger-than-life flat-screen TV. The learned professor is probably rolling over in her grave.

File under: residual Radcliffe

MASSACHUSETTS HALL

One restless spirit has taken the whole "pahk the cah in Hahvad Yahd" idiom quite literally…for almost a century. Massachusetts Hall has been the Ivy League's crown jewel, touted as the oldest building on the Cambridge campus and boasting a historical lineage that dates back to the country's second president, John Adams. For the record, he shared a triple room on the first floor in the 1750s. Its solid brick façade has been a symbol of American intelligentsia and has been the Yard's tacit sentinel for almost three centuries, dating back to 1720.

The Early Georgian–style dorm and office building, which currently houses freshmen on the top floor and served as a temporary barracks to 640 Continental soldiers during the Siege of Boston in the Revolutionary War, is also notoriously haunted. "Eighteenth-century buildings should have ghosts," mused William C. "Burriss" Young, who lived in Mass Hall for decades as an assistant dean of freshmen. "If there are going to be ghosts, it makes sense they should live in the nicest building in the Yard."

Harvard University's Massachusetts Hall had a resident ghost called Holbrook Smith, who was a "tall, respectable-looking older gentleman" known to chat up freshmen and claim to be among the class of 1914. *Photo by Ryan Miner.*

According to campus lore, the resident ghost known as Holbrook Smith was a "tall respectable-looking older gentleman" who would chat up freshmen and claim to be among the class of 1914. The strange gentleman was most active around the B entryway of Massachusetts Hall, where he often spooked students. "He was in his late fifties or early sixties—this was back in '67–'68—and he was dressed in wing-tipped shoes and a tweed jacket, very Ivy," described E. Fred Yalouris to the *Crimson*. "The man came into B entryway one day and knocked on our door. He proceeded to sit and talk, always 'very gracious and well-spoken.'" Young said Holbrook Smith "insisted that he had lived in B entry and that he had been roommates with Senator Saltonstall in the Class of 1914, but Senator Saltonstall had not lived in B entry."

Yalouris said Smith was "obviously an eccentric old gent" and he had the ability to "appear and disappear." The full-bodied apparition could travel through the building's brick façade. "One time he disappeared between the fourth and the first floor of the dorm," Yalouris said. "It was quite mysterious."

Smith returned to the dorm every fall for almost a century until Young confronted the so-called phantom and asked him to leave. He looked at the dean of freshmen with "the saddest eyes I've ever seen," recalled Young in an interview with *Harvard Magazine*, and said, "You've ruined a perfectly good thing."

Students and faculty have talked about hauntings at Harvard University's Massachusetts Hall for years. Thomas E. Crooks, a former administrator who passed away in 1998, told the *Harvard Crimson* in 1989 that "in Massachusetts Hall, there are a couple of ghosts who are passing as people." Crooks said that he had close encounters with spirits roaming the halls of Harvard. "Every time I see one, I forget it right away," Crooks said. "It's such a traumatic experience that I erase it from my mind at once."

Although Smith hasn't been seen roaming Mass Hall since that mythic confrontation, tour guides with Cambridge Haunts: Harvard Square Ghost Tour told the author that Smith's residual energy still lurks around the building. "He's made impromptu appearances on the tour and didn't like it when we talked about the way he looks," said tour guide Ashley Shakespeare, adding that he's a bit "uppity and protective" compared to other spirits on campus. In fact, several people who have taken photos of the building's exterior have captured odd orange light anomalies when Shakespeare alludes to Mass Hall's eccentric phantom. According to paranormal investigators, orange is a sign that an entity has assumed the role of a protector or caretaker. So, Smith may be serving as the building's otherworldly sentry.

In the late '70s, a noted clairvoyant visited the Massachusetts Hall dorm to investigate if residual spirits were indeed haunting Harvard's oldest building. "Students had expressed an interest in that sort of thing, and this lady had worked with the FBI in locating missing persons," Young recalled. "The speaker warned students that any photographs taken of her would not come out because of the strong supernatural presence in the room," reported the *Crimson*. "Sure enough, the photographs came out blank."

File under: spirit sentinel

THAYER HALL

Harvard Yard's most haunted? Some say Thayer Hall, built in 1870 and offered as a less-expensive housing alternative for the prestigious university's freshman population, is replete with full-bodied residual apparitions from a bygone era. Past residents include E.E. Cummings, Jordan's Prince Hamzah bi Al Hussein and Japan's Princess Owada Masako. However, campus ghost lore suggests that these high-profile undergrads weren't alone.

"They reportedly shared Thayer with the ghosts of a group of mill employees who once worked in the building when it was used as a textile mill," wrote Matthew L. Swayne, author of *America's Haunted Universities: Ghosts That Roam Hallowed Halls*. "Some people see the spirits outside walking into Thayer where there is no door. Those familiar with Thayer Hall say that some former entrances and exits were closed off when the building was reconditioned to become a dorm."

In fact, Thayer Hall made Hollow Hills' *Haunted New England Colleges* list in 2009. According to the website, spirits wearing Victorian-era clothing were spotted entering and leaving the building through doors that no longer exist. "A professor who chose to remain anonymous contacted me and said that he had seen Victorian figures going through areas in the hall where there used to be doors and there aren't now," said Fiona F. Broome, who came up with the most-haunted list. Broome told the *Crimson* that her source "was not a crazy person" and that "he had a lot of credibility. Just in the way that he wrote."

While Broome was convinced Thayer had a past life as a textile mill, there's no historical proof that the building served as a nineteenth-century

Thayer Hall made Hollow Hills' *Haunted New England Colleges* list in 2009. According to the website, spirits wearing Victorian-era clothing were spotted entering and leaving the building through doors that no longer exist. Contrary to reports, the dorm never had a previous life as a textile mill. *Photo by Ryan Miner.*

mill, and several residents have discredited the freshman legend as mere ghost lore. "I have seen no evidence of that so far," said Josh A. Bookin, a Thayer proctor, in an interview with the *Crimson*. "The most notable out of the ordinary activities are parties that need to be broken up."

Historically, Harvard freshmen have had a whimsical fascination with the spirit realm. In 1948, a group of eight men and three Radcliffe students formed an on-campus "spooks club." The group investigated a haunted mansion in Boston's Back Bay. Apparently, a high school teacher moved into the boarded-up estate in 1947 and had a run-in with an apparition. "They centered around the stairs," she told one of the club members. "Twice I saw a figure hovering there, and I was afraid to go upstairs." According to the report, the third time the phantom appeared, the woman asked, "Who's there?" and it disappeared.

So was the Thayer story conjured up by a group of freshmen with overactive imaginations? Perhaps. However, the dorm's ghost story can be traced back to 2002 to an encyclopedia of alleged haunts called *Haunted Places: The National Directory*. The book claimed that Thayer is "haunted by a half-dozen ghosts trying to get in from the outside," wrote Dennis William Hauck. "Thayer Hall used to be a textile mill and it is the spirits of former workers who are trying to get inside. Their apparitions, clad in period clothing, are seen late at night at the entrances." The book even suggested that "reports were most frequent during the winter months" but have decreased since "outdoor artificial light" was added outside Thayer's entrance.

After consulting with historians, the textile mill back story isn't true. In fact, looking at an 1856 map drawn under the direction of President Charles W. Eliot, the spot was just green space. Thayer Hall, the first of several dormitories built in the late 1800s, was sponsored by Nathaniel Thayer and was built to honor his Harvard alum father. It was never a textile mill. So it's more plausible that the freshman myth got its genesis from the *Haunted Places* listing. Harvard's most active? It's probably not Thayer.

However, many of the old-school buildings scattered throughout the Yard are hotbeds of alleged paranormal activity. There has also been a lot of construction near Thayer Hall, including a recently renovated basement, which could explain some recent reports of alleged paranormal activity. "The most active for me has been all the construction being done on Harvard's campus," said Ashley Shakespeare, tour guide with Cambridge Haunts, alluding to a two-year restoration of the building designed to make it more energy efficient and to reduce emissions. "I can't walk past any of the construction without getting an overwhelming feeling of spirit energy."

File under: Thayer myth

University Hall

Proof that not all alleged paranormal activity centers on the macabre, students who labored in the wee hours at Harvard's University Hall claimed that if you listen closely near the building's southwest entrance, you can hear a riotous residual haunting from the past. Yep, there have been reports of playful, disembodied voices replaying a legendary food fight when the building was a nineteenth-century dining hall. The white Chelmsford granite building, built between 1813 and 1815 by Harvard alum Charles Bulfinch, served as a massive first-floor dining hall known as the College Commons until it was partitioned into classrooms in 1849. The top floors boasted a chapel and library but were later reconditioned for the Faculty of Arts and Sciences.

According to ghost lore, there were "sounds of a phantom dinner party that filled the corridor by the southwest corner of University Hall, a displaced echo of the dining hall that occupied the building in the 19th century," confirmed the *Crimson*. Apparently, the food fight was so over the top that it left a psychic imprint on the historic hall. It's what is known as a spirit-level recording, or residual haunting, that replays over and over again like a videotape. "How and why past events are recorded and replayed repetitiously is not understood," speculated Lauren Forcella of the Paranormal Network. "Whatever the actual mechanism, it apparently possesses longevity as the encore performances of a haunting can continue for decades or longer. Generally, the haunting is a fragment or portion of an actual event."

On November 1, 1818, students assembled for a peaceful Sunday dinner at University Hall. "Then all hell broke loose," wrote the *Harvard*

Students who worked in University Hall claimed that if you listen closely at the southwest entrance, you can hear the disembodied voices from beyond replaying a legendary food fight from when the building was a nineteenth-century dining hall. *Courtesy of the Library of Congress.*

Gazette. "A major food fight set off a cascade of disturbances, and within one week the entire sophomore class was expelled." It's known as the "Rebellion of 1818."

The College Commons dining hall was an open space, and reportedly the design "made it easy for students eventually to throw food, furniture and handy projectiles at rival classes. The adjoining chambers, wrote one contemporary, were like barrels of gunpowder stacked side by side." Someone threw a slice of buttered bread, which led to a full-blown food fight. Weapons of class destruction included teacups, plates and wood. The entire sophomore class, which included literary icon Ralph Waldo Emerson, was expelled after a series of protests and gatherings around what was known as the "protest tree." Of course, a majority of the eighty students, including Emerson, were reinstated.

The seeds of protest were firmly planted in the soil surrounding University Hall. In 1834, a group of freshmen found President Josiah Quincy III's iron fist enforcing rules unreasonable. So they torched a classroom, set off an explosion in Holden Chapel and hanged Quincy in effigy—from the branches of the protest tree no doubt—which led to campus-wide revolt.

Many believe the rambunctious voices of protest continue to haunt Harvard's University Hall. However, some ghost lore experts claim the sounds from the phantom food fight disappeared in the late 1960s. Perhaps Harvard's Vietnam-era counterculture set the ghosts of the school's rebellious past free?

William C. "Burriss" Young, who lived in nearby Mass Hall as an assistant dean of freshmen and was known as a "veritable font of Harvard ghost lore," claimed that the spirited disembodied voices magically disappeared, pointing out that "no one has heard it since 'the bust.'" For the record, "the bust" referred to when students took over the hall in 1969 and occupied it for eighteen hours in protest of Harvard's stance on the Vietnam War. Massachusetts state police broke down the historic building's front doors to get in while they removed the hippie troublemakers. Young said that "since then, either the ghosts have been so distraught at the police breaking up the party or the breaking of the doors ruined something in the acoustics of the place, but no one's heard anything."

File under: phantom protests

WELD HALL

Stressed-out college kids and ghost stories? It's a no-brainer. However, the elaborate tales weaved in the hallowed halls of Harvard transcend the "little girl ghost who fell down an elevator shaft" norm. Weld Hall, built by Memorial Hall designers Ware & Van Brunt in 1870 and featuring a Hogwarts-style Queen Anne façade, has a decades-old legend. According to Margaret John, the dorm's proctor in the 1980s, "a spirit was bricked in between the walls" when the hall was refurbished as a precaution against fire in the 1960s. "Students often hear mysterious knocking on the walls," she continued.

For the record, Weld has a history of housing creative alums ranging from John F. Kennedy to author Michael Crichton. The dorm's two creepy towers, boasting a clerestory (or Roman basilica–type window structure designed to let in natural lighting), were blocked off to prevent accidents, but they have inspired stories of phantom knockings and, more notably, an encounter with "an old woman with a dark cloak and grayish hair" in 1985. Yep, one freaked-out freshman swore she saw a ghost in the Weld North common room.

"We were sitting in a circle around a little red candle left over from Hurricane Gloria. The windows were open, there was a full moon and we were feeling deeply relaxed," said Audris S. Wong in an interview with the *Crimson*. "My eyes were transfixed on the space between my two roommates, when I saw an old woman with a dark cloak and grayish hair."

Wong, who refused to talk about the incident when approached by the school newspaper the following year, described the alleged full-bodied apparition in detail. "It wasn't like the mist that you see in the movies," she recalled, "but it was very vague—like an impression. I couldn't see any of her features. She was just leaning against the wall, listening to our conversation."

The freshman's classmate backed up Wong's account, although she didn't see the cloak-wearing school spirit because her view was blocked. "It was a really mellow atmosphere," she said. "Audris suddenly stopped the conversation and told us, in a calm voice, that the ghost was there."

According to the article, the nineteenth-century building had a history of supernatural shenanigans. "Weld Hall's reputation as the center of Harvard's occult has been revived by the sighting of a ghost in one of its rooms," the story contends, although another Weld North student brushed off the incident, saying the students were "probably intoxicated" and "there are no such things as ghosts."

One student swore she saw "an old woman with a dark cloak and grayish hair" in Weld North in 1985. Featuring a Hogwarts-style Queen Anne façade, there's also ghost lore suggesting that a spirit was bricked in between the structure's walls. *Photo by Ryan Miner.*

Meanwhile, that same year, an Eliot House junior swore she saw a shadow figure in the building's I-entry room but later recanted the story. "She said she sensed a presence and saw a specter, but it was really brief," reported the ghost-seer's roommate. "She said it was not a fearful presence." The unidentified Eliot House junior said, "I went from a light place to a dark place, and I saw an image, but it was probably just my eyes adjusting," she concluded. "I don't believe in ghosts."

Harvard's hot-and-cold fascination with the supernatural dates back hundreds of years. In fact, there's one particular yarn from 1846 attributed to artist Washington Allston that serves as a cautionary tale of sorts for those fixated with the paranormal. "Old Harvard, in our time, though frequently troubled with spirits, suffered no annoyance whatever with ghosts," wrote Felix Octavius Carr Darley in *Ghost Stories*. "Science and unbelief had frightened them all away," he mused. "Still, however, there lingered some old traditions of ghosts, in former times, who had made these classic shades their haunts—ghosts real and fictitious."

Allston, who graduated from Harvard College in 1800, talked about an old college prank gone terribly awry. In the legend, an eighteenth-century troublemaker decided to dress in white and sneak into his roommate's chambers in an attempt to convince him that ghosts exist. The unaware student, who kept a pistol under his pillow, confronted the so-called spirit, took aim and shot at the ghostly intruder. He didn't know that the roommate had removed the bullets from his gun. "When the smoke cleared away—there stood the grim figure, as before, immovable and apparently invulnerable."

According to the tall tale, the roommate was immediately struck with fear and panicked over the idea that he was face to face with a ghost. The gun-toting student fell to the ground and started to convulse, which led to a series of seizures. According to Allston's story, the freaked-out Harvard student died.

True tale? Perhaps. The moral of the story is that "the mind of man is too delicate and complicated a structure to be tampered with by experiments of this description," the story concludes, adding that it's "dangerous to counterfeit any thing of this kind for the purpose of producing terror in the mind of another." Meanwhile, students at Weld continue to hear mysterious knocks echoing throughout their old-school hall.

File under: freshman fear

CHAPTER 4

HOLY HAUNTS

What happens to us after we die may not be an issue for a person of faith; however, there's a subconscious desire to know that life exists after death. Not surprisingly, religion is chock-full of spine-tingling tales involving the supernatural. "In the Bible, the story of King Saul calling on the witch of Endor to summon the spirit of Samuel has been recorded, and have the questions surrounding whether Jesus after his resurrection was a living being or a ghost," wrote Otto Penzler in *The Big Book of Ghost Stories*. "From ancient texts in Greek mythology, various types of ghosts are described in Homer's *Iliad* and *Odyssey*, and Romans, notably Plutarch and Pliny the Younger, wrote about haunted houses."

Ghost lore involving religious enclaves? Yep, Cambridge has its share of holy haunts.

While people find solace in these places of worship, the emotions associated with important events—like a marriage or a baptism—can linger within these hallowed and often historic walls. "In some Catholic churches, for example, nuns and priests devote their entire lives to serving the church and spend countless hours each week in prayer, teaching or maintaining their church as part of their devotion to God," explained tour guide Beth Rupert in *Witchita Haunts*. "It is believed this energy and these repetitive actions can be captured as a residual haunt in a church."

There are also controversial events—like interring British soldier lieutenant Richard Brown within Christ Church's Vassall tomb—that could leave a psychic imprint of sorts on a building. Apparently, thousands of angry Patriots ransacked the Anglican church in protest of Brown's burial, and their anti-Loyalist sentiment could have left a supernatural imprint on the structure.

Of course, many of New England's meetinghouses boast nearby cemeteries, and Cambridge is no exception. The allegedly haunted Christ Church, rumored to be haunted by the fallen British soldier, boasts the second-oldest burying ground in the city. It's also rumored to be its most haunted.

"People are fascinated with cemeteries," explained Jim McCabe in a 2007 interview with the *Boston Herald*. "It's like going to a historical house. The rest of the country just doesn't have the sense of history we do."

Adam Berry from *Ghost Hunters* believes that "the older the cemetery, the more intimidating." Cambridge's Old Burying Ground, dating back to the early 1600s, is no exception to the rule. In fact, Berry said that it's highly plausible that the cemetery has residual energy simply because it's been around for centuries.

But is Cambridge's Old Burying Ground haunted? Perhaps. Berry believes that some spirits return to their graves even after passing almost three centuries ago. "Cemeteries are where they go to rest and don't want to be bothered. I don't believe they're bound or held captive in that specific spot. However, I do feel they're abundant."

So if you're looking for haunted churches, also check their nearby burial grounds.

In contrast, Cambridge's less ancient Mount Auburn Cemetery, home turf of New England's most wanted, including senator and abolitionist Charles Sumner and University Hall architect Charles Bulfinch, is apparently not haunted. "There is no known ghost lore surrounding Mount Auburn Cemetery," confirmed Stephanie Gillette, the cemetery's external affairs coordinator. "People tend to impose ideas of the kinds of stories that they think should exist here, but unfortunately they have no merit."

For example, there's a spooky tale involving John Wilkes Booth's brother, Edwin, that has surfaced on a few Halloween-themed tours. According to one ghost lore enthusiast, the fallen actor's spirit reportedly hangs out at the cemetery's Story Chapel. "It would be very romantic to believe that the ghost of Edwin Booth is milling around in our chapels, but as a staff person who spends a lot of time in both chapels by herself at all times of day and night, I can confidently say that I have never encountered a spirit," continued Gillette. "The same goes for staff who have been here for more than forty years."

A ghostly tale involving John Wilkes Booth's brother, Edwin, surfaced claiming that the fallen actor's spirit hangs out at the Mount Auburn Cemetery's picturesque Story Chapel. Not true, remarked a spokesperson for the cemetery, adding that the rumor has "no merit." *Courtesy of the Library of Congress.*

Built in 1831 by wealthy Bostonians and boasting 175 acres of rolling hills, Mount Auburn Cemetery claims to be exempt from the haunted cemetery theory. However, I've assembled a spirited crew of atypical holy haunts, ranging from Harvard's Holden Chapel, which reportedly boasts a female spirit that makes a postmortem return during the first snowfall, to an allegedly cursed church in Cambridgeport. It gives new meaning to "holy spirit."

CAMBRIDGEPORT BAPTIST CHURCH

The seventeenth-century witch hysteria serves as a modern cautionary tale casting a dark shadow on the dangers of religious extremism and the importance of due process. While Salem's series of hearings and prosecutions from February 1692 to May 1693 continues to cast a spell on the masses, Cambridge and Boston were bitten by the mob malady as well, and many of the same finger pointers, including Reverend Cotton Mather, perpetuated a similar frenzy in the small villages throughout New England's blood-soaked landscape.

Witch hunts? Yep, Cambridge had them too.

The Newtowne Market jail was built between Winthrop Square and Eliot Street (currently home to Staples and the restaurant called Park) in 1692 when the witch-hunt mentality started to sweep New England. Many women who were accused of cavorting with evil and Quakers like Anne Hutchinson were imprisoned there but never hanged. Some, like Lydia Dustin, who was declared not guilty of the dark arts but couldn't afford the prison fees, died tragically in shackles. In contrast, Dustin's relative Elizabeth Coleson was

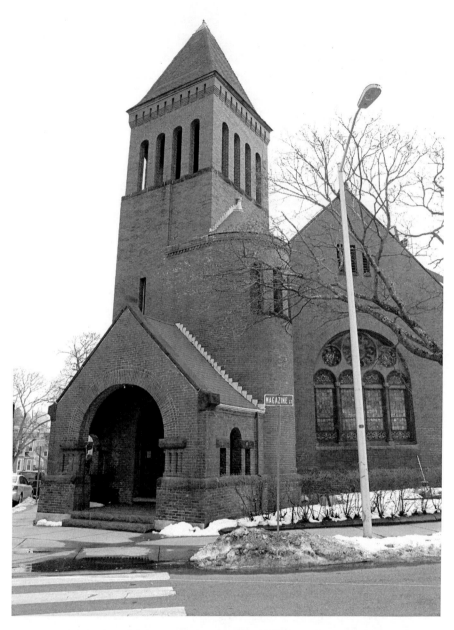

There's a historic ghost story associated with Cambridgeport Baptist Church after it burned down in 1881. Locals reported hearing cries of agony, moans and shrieks. According to legend, a colonial-era woman known as Ann Hopkins was burned at the spot of the church and screamed as she was engulfed in flames, "The curse of fire shall be upon this spot forever!" *Photo by Ryan Miner.*

also accused and found not guilty of so-called evil. She was released several days before her grandmother's tragic death on March 10, 1693.

Boston's alleged witches, like Ann "Goody" Glover, weren't as lucky. Glover, a self-sufficient, strong-willed Irishwoman who spoke fluent Gaelic, lived in the North End, where she washed laundry for John Goodwin and his family. After a spirited spat in her native Gaelic tongue with Goodwin's thirteen-year-old daughter, Martha, Glover was accused of bewitching the four children in the household and was sent to prison for practicing the dark arts. Reverend Cotton Mather, who was a major player in Salem's trials, wrote that Glover was a "scandalous old Irishwoman, very poor, a Roman Catholic and obstinate in idolatry." During her trial, Glover was asked to recite the Lord's Prayer. Speaking in broken English, she only knew the Catholic, rather than the Puritan Protestant, version of the prayer. She was hanged from the Great Elm in the Boston Common on November 16, 1688. Glover was one of four women who were accused, and executed, for witchcraft in Boston over a forty-year period beginning with the execution of Margaret Jones in 1648.

While a majority of Cambridge's alleged witches avoided the gallows, there's one tall tale from the city's not-so-Puritanical past involving Cambridgeport's Ann Hopkins. "The Cambridgeport Baptist Church, where Magazine Street ends in Central Square, burned down in 1881," reported the *Boston Globe*. "Residents reported hearing cries of agony, low moans and shrieks that disappeared in the wind. Legend has it that back in colonial days, a local woman who lived alone, Ann Hopkins, was burned at the spot of the church. As she burned, she screamed, 'The curse of fire shall be upon this spot forever!'"

The Cambridgeport Baptist Church legend surrounding a supposed vigilante witch burning surfaced in 1881 in an article called "Ann Hopkins' Ghost" published in the *Boston Daily Globe*. The church, founded in the 1800s, burned down twice and was rebuilt in 1868. Construction workers noticed that "a spark of fire was struck out in some unaccountable way" when a large stone was unearthed. An older gentleman recounted the legend dating back to the "early days of the Massachusetts colony when witches were burned and Quakers were hanged." According to the tale, Hopkins was once "the most beautiful girl in the settlement" and became a recluse after being jilted by a lover. "This was the blow that unsettled her reason and made her shun the society of mankind," he said. "As time rolled on and her sad story was forgotten, her cabin came to be regarded as the abode of evil spirits and children were taught to avoid the malign influence of her gaze."

During the witch hysteria, Hopkins was blamed for the death of a cow that gave bloody milk. During a major thunderstorm in the late 1600s, a local reported seeing "strange lights and unholy noises" coming from Hopkins's Cambridgeport cabin, and one woman swore she saw Hopkins pass her window on a broomstick.

Hopkins was accused of witchcraft and allegedly burned at the stake by a group of vigilantes. Her dying words? "The curse of fire shall be upon this spot forever!" she supposedly uttered as she raised her "blackened right arm toward heaven." The reporter, pointing out the mysterious church fire in 1868, believed Hopkins's spirit haunted the church. "Who can say that it is not her spirit that haunts the place?" the reporter mused. "The curse of Ann Hopkins is here today."

According to the Cambridge legend, the disembodied moans and reported "cries of agony" diminished when the church was rebuilt. But is her story true? Historians believe the Hopkins tale is a possible hyperbolic retelling of an actual case involving Harvard Square–area colonial women.

On June 1, 1659, magistrate Thomas Danforth signed a warrant to arrest widow Winifred Holman and her daughter Mary "on suspicion of witchcraft." The two women lived on the northwest corner of the Cambridge Common, on Garden Street, and their neighbors, the Gibson family, became convinced that their married daughter, Rebecca Stearns, was enchanted by the widow and her daughter, who offered herbs to cure ailments.

While pregnant, Stearns experienced "two extraordinary strange fits," wrote Diane Rapaport in *The Naked Quaker*, which seemed to be exacerbated when Mary trekked over to the Gibson home to "borrow fire" to rekindle the Holman hearth. Stearns, during one of her *Exorcist*-esque rages that involved barking like a dog, accused Holman of being a witch. Danforth, who grew up with the Holmans, reluctantly signed an order accusing the women of witchcraft after Stearns's unborn child died. The case went to trial in 1660, and the Holman women were found not guilty and Stearns was ruled "mentally incompetent."

Ironically, Danforth's post-Cambridge judicial career flourished, and he became a judge at the Salem witchcraft trials in the late 1600s. No word on what happened to the widow Holman and her daughter after the accusations and subsequent trial. However, the Ann Hopkins legend and Mary Holman's quest for fire are somewhat similar. Perhaps the alleged stake burning of Hopkins in Cambridgeport was a distorted retelling of the Holman case somehow twisted over time.

File under: fire starter

CHRIST CHURCH

Wanna hobnob with the ghosts of Cambridge's historical past? Built in 1759, Christ Church has hosted a slew of the country's luminaries, ranging from George and Martha Washington, who rallied to save the building from neglect, to Teddy Roosevelt, who taught Sunday school while studying at Harvard. In 1968, Martin Luther King Jr. and Dr. Benjamin Spock held a press conference in the structure's Parish Hall and formally announced their support for the antiwar movement and their opposition to the Vietnam War.

The oldest church in Cambridge, with a history spanning more than 250 years, Christ Church is rumored to be haunted by a British soldier. "He was buried under the church after being thrown from a wagon," reported *Cambridge Day* in 2005. "The church was considered Tory, sympathetic to the British cause during the American Revolution, and the ghost wanders the pews looking for his regiment."

Many of the church's founders lived on Tory Row, now called Brattle Street. Christ Church's initial mission was "to minister to English families in

The oldest church in Cambridge, with a history spanning more than 250 years, Christ Church located at Zero Garden Street is rumored to be haunted by a British soldier who occasionally reveals himself and blows out candles. *Courtesy of the Library of Congress.*

Cambridge and students at Harvard." The British rented out box pews at the Anglican church, and as the Revolutionary War waged on, the chapel was closed until 1790. It was renovated in 1883 and then restored to its original design in 1920. The Harvard Square church, located at Zero Garden Street, is a Cambridge anachronism, looking as it did during the mid-eighteenth century. Incidentally, it was attacked by angry Patriots because of its Tory leanings, and the church's organ was melted and turned into bullets during the war.

The ghost story centers on the Battle of Saratoga in 1777, when Christ Church was reopened for the internment of English and German prisoners known as the Convention Troops. Apparently, neither the locals nor the administration at Harvard College wanted anything to do with the imprisoned British redcoats. However, hundreds of foreign soldiers wandered the streets of Cambridge and were imprisoned later as the war blazed on in New England.

In June 1778, a British redcoat known as Lieutenant Richard Brown lost control of his horse-drawn carriage while descending Prospect Hill in Somerville. According to E. Ashley Rooney's *Cambridge, Massachusetts: Ghosts, Legends & Lore*, Brown was stopped by an American sentry, who pulled out his gun at the frazzled soldier. Brown pointed to his sword, which indicated his rank and privilege. The sentry shot Brown in the head, and he was buried on June 19, 1778, at the only church in town where Americans and British worshiped together. He was interred with military honors in the Vassall tomb vault many feet beneath the church.

The spirit haunting Christ Church is rumored to be Brown. "The ghost of British Lieutenant Richard Brown is thought to still walk about the sanctuary," wrote Rooney. "Visitors may see that the candles are suddenly extinguished and hear odd shuffling noises and doors bang—yet no one is there."

Former church archivist Donna LaRue, in the October 31, 1986 edition of the *Harvard Crimson*, echoed the ghostly rumors. "He comes up once in a while and blows out candles," she said.

File under: holy ghost

HOLDEN CHAPEL

Holden Chapel, which was used as the first cadaver room when the college hosted the Harvard Medical College, is rumored to be teeming with ghosts from its past. Built in 1744, the Colonial-style building was the spiritual

Built in 1774, Holden Chapel was used as Harvard's first cadaver room when it was the hub of the college's burgeoning medical school. The colonial structure reportedly boasts a female spirit that returns every year during the first snowstorm looking for the skeletal remains of her lover. She hasn't been spotted since human bones were recovered during an excavation in 1999. *Photo by Ryan Miner.*

gathering place as well as a secular lecture hall for Harvard students until 1772. The chapel housed 160 soldiers from 1775 to 1776 in the days leading up to the American Revolution. It later become the hub of Harvard's burgeoning medical school, established in 1783 by John Warren, and served as a morgue for students in training for half a century.

One legend alludes to Holden Chapel's macabre medical history. According to the late William C. "Burriss" Young, who lived in nearby Mass Hall as an assistant dean of freshmen, there's a female spirit that returns to Holden Chapel every year "around the first snowstorm." Her name? Pickham. According to Young, she was "a woman who was riding with her fiancé in a sleigh through the square when their horse slipped on the ice and their sleigh flipped over. Her fiancé broke his neck and died in her arms." According to the legend, he was buried at the Old Burying Ground, but "when she returned to visit the grave, the body had been dug up and stolen."

Back in the day, resurrection men—or grave robbers—would keep careful track of who died and where they were buried. When there was an opportunity to sell a body to a medical school, the resurrection man would go and dig up someone recently deceased. It was common practice for people like Ephraim Littlefield, who was a janitor at the Harvard Medical School and rumored to be a grave robber, to retrieve a dead body when the medical school's stock of cadavers was getting low.

The female spirit that allegedly haunts Holden Chapel "became convinced that her fiancé's body was in Holden Chapel, which housed the dissecting labs at that time," continued Young. "Every year, at the first snowstorm, she would escape from her family's house in New Bedford and try to break into Holden Chapel and would have to be physically restrained from entering. She's still spotted from time to time," Young told the *Crimson* in 1997. "And if you ever see her, and you observe carefully, you'll notice that she doesn't leave any footprints in the snow."

The medical school moved in the 1800s from Harvard Yard to Boston, where one of its famous alums, Dr. John Webster, was accused of what was called the crime of the century: the murder of Dr. George Parkman. It's likely that Webster and Parkman made their first contact at Holden Chapel in the early nineteenth century.

Dr. Parkman was beaten and dismembered in a Harvard Medical College laboratory in 1849. Based on a bizarre plumbing accident that occurred on November 23, 1999, exactly 150 years after Parkman's macabre murder, his spirit is rumored to haunt the house that bears his family name. It faces the Boston Common and is located at 33 Beacon Street. Also, the

Parkman Bandstand, located in the center of the public park and erected posthumously, stands as a solemn reminder of one of the most talked about trials of the 1800s.

It's a tale of a $400 loan turned deadly.

Hailing from one of the most prominent families in Boston, Parkman was a retired doctor who became a landlord and money lender in the early 1800s. Nicknamed "old chin," Parkman befriended one of his clients, John White Webster, who was a professor of chemistry and geology at Harvard Medical College. Incidentally, the Parkman family donated a large sum of money to fund the Harvard's medical school's move to Boston from its former location near the Mass General Hospital.

Webster borrowed $400 from Parkman, who was reported missing days following an attempt to collect his money. Bostonians were on the hunt for the missing landlord, and police printed twenty-eight thousand missing-person fliers. After a sensational trial and Webster's eventual confession, the press had a field day spitting out "Harvard Professor and Murderer" headlines guaranteed to captivate the city. On August 30, 1850, the professor was hanged at the gallows.

How did Webster murder Parkman? After an unexpected collections call at Webster's laboratory, the professor took his walking stick and clubbed Parkman in the head during a momentary fit of rage. Panicked, Webster reportedly chopped up the body into pieces and threw the remains into the privy, also known as a toilet.

In his confession, Webster claimed that it was an act of self-defense. He said that Parkman "was speaking and gesticulating in the most violent and menacing manner" about the loan. In response, Webster "seized whatever thing was handiest—it was a stick of wood—and dealt him an instantaneous blow with all the force that passion could give it. It was on the side of his head, and there was nothing to break the force of the blow. He fell instantly upon the pavement. There was no second blow. He did not move."

During the trial, a police officer testified that Parkman's torso was found in a bloodstained tea chest, which was displayed to the court. Webster also allegedly burned Parkman's bones, including his jawbone replete with false teeth, in the furnace. The officer also said that it was possible to fit the victim's remaining body parts in the toilet, but the torso wouldn't fit.

With such a macabre legacy, Holden Chapel today looks like a throwback to Harvard's days of yore. For most of the twentieth century, it hosted the Harvard Glee Club and later the Radcliffe Choral Society. The chapel was renovated in 1999, and archaeologists discovered human remains in the building's basement. "My first thought was, 'Oooohh, an old Harvard murder,'" said Associate Professor of Anthropology Carole A.S. Mandryk in a '99 *Crimson* interview. "They're definitely human bones." According to the report, workers found several sawed-open skeletons, broken scientific glassware and test tubes strewn among the remains. "Between 1782 and 1850, part of the basement was used as an anatomy and dissection lecture hall for the Medical School," wrote the *Crimson*. "Some of the bones have metal pieces sticking out of them, as if someone was trying to construct a skeleton," Mandryk added.

Remember the wailing female spirit known as Pickham that returns to Holden Chapel during the first snowstorm? She hasn't been spotted since the building's renovations. It's possible that she was right and her fiancé's remains were buried in the basement. Perhaps Pickham finally got some postmortem closure when the bones were unearthed and removed from Holden Chapel.

File under: Holden's skeletons

CHAPTER 5

LANDMARK HAUNTS

C ambridge is a hotbed of paranormal activity. Whether you're a believer or not, there are more than a few skeletons in the city's collective closet. Many of those three-hundred-year-old secrets can be found in the buildings and landmarks scattered throughout the historic city. In fact, many of the spirits allegedly lingering in Cambridge might be a byproduct of the strong-willed New England desire to maintain the old buildings of the past, which act as lures to both visitors and ghosts. "Spirits are attracted to the places they lived in," opined the late Jim McCabe, who was a noted paranormal expert in the region. "I think what attracts ghosts up here is that you don't tear down the buildings."

Adam Berry, winner of Syfy's *Ghost Hunters Academy* and a noted paranormal investigator from *Ghost Hunters*, echoed McCabe's theory. "Because of the history, there are so many interesting places that could be investigated. It [Cambridge] had tons of activity during the Revolutionary and Civil Wars. There must be spirits left behind, mulling about and checking out the status of the community they built way back when." During his four-year collegiate stint at the Boston Conservatory, the famed paranormal investigator said he fell in love with the city. "Its rich history and the singular fact that it was the cornerstone of the American Revolution makes it a city that is truly one of a kind," Berry said. "Why would anyone want to leave...even after they're dead?"

One Harvard Square oddity, the *Harvard Lampoon* building, was erected in 1909 and looks like a mock Flemish castle. The structure, located at 44

Built in 1909, the *Harvard Lampoon* building houses the oldest U.S. humor magazine and looks like a mock Flemish castle. The landmark's curator claims the Harvard Square oddity has a resident male ghost that walks the halls and is seen by many people. *Photo by Ryan Miner.*

Bow Street, houses the oldest humor magazine in the United States and is also reportedly inhabited by a male spirit with an enduring sense of humor. Curator Joe Hickey told *Cambridge Day* that his team has no clue who the ghost is—the spirit is a supposedly a male figure who walks the castle's labyrinthine halls and has been spotted by many people. "It's the creepiest building to be in when you're alone at night," he said.

The oldest standing house in Cambridge is the colonial-era Cooper-Frost-Austin House, which is believed to have been constructed in 1681. Tucked away in North Cambridge's Avon Hill, the lean-to "half house" was built by Samuel Cooper, a deacon of First Church and a town selectman from 1704 to 1716. Cooper bequeathed the property to his son Walter, who extended the west end of the home in 1718. Currently operated by Historic New England and not open to the public, the Linnaean Street haunt was handed down the Cooper family tree for 250 years.

While people who have visited the Cooper-Frost-Austin House say it's a creaky old building that boasts an eerie haunted house aesthetic, historians say the ghosts of Avon Hill lurk in the area surrounding the historic hot spot. Cambridge's execution place, known as Gallows Hill, where hundreds of people were killed for various crimes, is a stone's throw from the Linnaean Street house.

"It's a creepy place," said Gavin Kleespies, executive director of the Cambridge Historical Society, adding that the actual location is a private parking lot known as Stone Court, located near 15–19 Lancaster Street. "It's right behind the shops, like Joie de Vivre, on Massachusetts Avenue," he added. Kleespies's predecessor, historian Thomas Francis O'Malley, wrote in 1923 that the place of execution "was located upon the common land a bit removed from the more thickly settled part of the community. It is perhaps not too much to say that all of the executions ordered in Middlesex County took place on this lot until 1817." There was also an ominous relic marking the spot: a sign reading "The Way to Gallows Hill" posted on the corner of Massachusetts Avenue that stood as a tacit reminder of the horrors of Cambridge's not-so-Puritanical past.

As far as notable executions, Kleespies said Goody Elizabeth Kendall, who was accused of witchcraft, was wrongly tortured to death at Gallows Hill in the seventeenth century. The historian said the most horrific account occurred in 1755. "Mark and Phillis, two slaves accused of poisoning Captain John Codman, a Charlestown merchant whose 'rigid discipline' they had found 'unendurable,' were executed," Kleespies recounted in the historical society's newsletter. "Phillis, as was customary, was strangled and her body burned. Mark was hanged and his body suspended in irons on a gibbet along what is now Washington Street in Somerville, near the Charlestown line." Mark was put into a cage to decompose near the current Holiday Inn on Somerville's Washington Street as a public reminder of his crime. Paul Revere, who rode past twenty years later, mentioned it in his accounts of his midnight ride. Phillis, on the other hand, was savagely burned at the stake.

According to several sources, many of the homes and former Lesley College buildings surrounding Gallows Hill are teeming with the tortured spirits from Cambridge's Gallows Hill past. "Phenomena include disembodied footsteps and objects that move by themselves," wrote Dennis William Hauck in *Haunted Places: The National Directory*. Also, the *Boston Globe* reported that Phillis's cries can be heard echoing throughout Avon Hill. "They say, if you listen closely on a windy day, you can still hear her screaming as she went up in smoke," said tour guide Daniel Berger-Jones.

In addition to the inexplicable sounds and shadows, there are reports of a female specter wearing colonial-era attire, weeping and sometimes shrieking. Adam Berry said it's possible that the residual energy surrounding the Gallows Hill site is left behind from the public executions. In the past, Berry said that he's heard "reports of women wailing or crying. They're in grief. It's possible that something traumatic has happened and they've died or they're searching for their son or soldier."

Or perhaps it's Phillis posthumously begging for justice and setting the record straight about the slave master she may—or may not—have murdered with arsenic.

KIRKLAND STREET NIGHTMARE

You've heard of *The Amityville Horror*? Well, Cambridge had its own version known as the "Kirkland Street Nightmare." The Treadwell-Sparks House located at 21 Kirkland Street was originally built in 1838 and was moved from Quincy Street to its current location in 1968. However, the house that stood there before had a haunted history that made headlines in the *Boston Daily Globe* on April 8, 1878.

Over a fifteen-year span, tenants at the original house would come and go without giving any explanation. There were reports of disembodied voices, and after a series of revolving-door dwellers, the double-decker was abandoned for years because of its "haunted house" reputation.

The Treadwell-Sparks House located at 21 Kirkland Street was moved to land that was reportedly haunted by a teen spirit known as Bertha who terrorized a family in 1878. The story made headlines in the late 1800s, and the horrors that allegedly occurred in the house were "enough to frighten people to death." *Photo by Ryan Miner.*

College students threw rocks through the windows, and stressed-out Harvard kids would squat at the dilapidated house for a spooky night out. In 1878, a man described as Mr. Marsh and his family rented the homestead for fifteen dollars a month and shrugged off the rumors that the house was haunted.

Soon, Marsh started hearing his name called out by a demonic, disembodied voice. He also watched in horror as the handle of his door slowly turned and opened when no one, at least among the living, was in the room. After close encounters with an unseen force, the man organized a Victorian-style séance. During the spiritual intervention, Marsh's wife allegedly became possessed by the so-called spirit haunting the house. Mrs. Marsh described in detail the story of an orphan girl who was forcibly taken into the home by a carriage where she was, according to the report, "foully dealt with, murdered and buried in the cellar below the house." During the séance, the spirit said her name was Bertha.

After a few months without paranormal activity, the house's freaked-out tenants started hearing odd noises in the home and up the stairs. They also heard the sounds of glass shattering in the kitchen, yet nothing was broken. The maid claimed she heard "terrible noises" at night and said the furniture in the room was pushed by invisible hands. She also recalled hearing blood-curdling shrieks and cries from a female voice.

After the initial article called "The Spook Roost" appeared in the *Globe*, former residents recalled seeing a full-bodied apparition of a young girl. They recounted objects, like plates on the kitchen table, moving when no one was there. Hundreds of curious spectators gathered around the Kirkland Street house at night while Mr. Marsh dug in the cellar to find the remains of the supposedly murdered girl known as Bertha.

Bones were found in the basement. However, a former tenant claimed that he would bury slaughtered animal bones in the cellar. Investigators couldn't tell if the remains were human or animal. In 1878, police didn't have the forensic and DNA tools investigators use today.

The Marshes, after undergoing public scrutiny because of the reports in the *Globe*, stopped talking to the press and demanded privacy. After several years, they fled the haunted house on Kirkland Street, and it was eventually demolished.

A former maid, Mary Nolan, confirmed the alleged haunting to the *Globe*. "Often I heard the carriage drive up, stop and then go on again. Why, that was quite common. We would hear the sound of wheels, the hoofs of the horses and sometimes the crack of the whip but nothing could be seen. I wouldn't live in that house again for $1,000," Nolan said. "It was enough to frighten people to death."

The late Reverend Peter Gomes, a prominent Harvard theologian and author who lived in the Treadwell-Sparks House until his passing, commented about the ghost lore surrounding Divinity Hall. The Kirkland Street house is near Harvard Divinity. "It was said that if you heard strange noises by the chapel or saw someone there you didn't recognize, it was probably a ghost," Gomes said, adding that the spirits were believed to be "benign, doubtless Unitarian, rational ghosts." Gomes never commented on the female spirit allegedly haunting his home on Kirkland Street.

William James—a Harvard luminary and founder of the American Society for Psychical Research, which is one of the oldest organizations exploring the paranormal—lived at 95 Irving Street, which is a stone's throw from the Kirkland Street haunt. His first essay for the society was about a girl who mysteriously vanished from her home in Enfield, New Hampshire. James investigated the haunting premonitions of Nellie Titus, who allegedly predicted how the sixteen-year-old died on Halloween in the late 1800s. According to the essay, Titus strongly believed that the girl drowned near a Shaker-style bridge in Enfield. Her body was found, but the case continues to be a mystery.

The dead girl's name? Bertha Huse.

File under: lonely bones

MEMORIAL HALL

Based purely on aesthetics, Harvard's Memorial Hall looks haunted. The gothic, high-Victorian structure was erected in honor of graduates who fought for the Union in the American Civil War. According to author and alum Henry James, Memorial Hall consists of three divisions: "One of them a theater, for academic ceremonies; another a vast refectory, covered with a timbered roof, hung about with portraits and lighted by stained windows, like the halls of the colleges of Oxford; and the third, the most interesting, a chamber high, dim and severe, consecrated to the sons of the university who fell in the long Civil War," James wrote in *The Bostonians*.

The breakdown, according to James, is Sanders Theater, Annenberg Hall (which boasts the massive Harry Potter–esque dining hall) and the Memorial Transept. Beneath Annenberg Hall is Loker Commons, which hosts music practice rooms and an upperclassmen lunch area. The Transept boasts an awe-inspiring sixty-foot-high gothic vault replete with stunning stained-glass windows and twenty-eight tablets commemorating the 136 Harvard men who died fighting in the Civil War. Oddly, the 71 Harvard graduates from the South who fought for the Confederacy aren't included in the memorial.

This controversial omission is at the core of the spirits allegedly haunting Memorial Hall. Ashley Shakespeare, a tour guide with Cambridge Haunts and self-proclaimed ghost magnet, said he's seen a full-bodied apparition peeking out of the doorway during several of his tours. "What I feel he has told me is that he was one of the students from Harvard that fought in the Civil War and ended up being killed in battle, never being able to return to Harvard and finish his education," Shakespeare said. "He wanted to leave a legacy, but his life was taken away abruptly. He had dreams and ambitions, and he's thrilled that now through the tour we have given him a voice and a legacy."

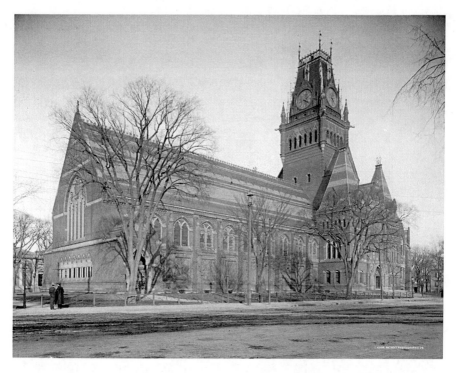

Memorial Hall, built to commemorate the 136 Harvard men who died fighting in the Civil War, is reportedly haunted by a Confederate soldier who left campus during Harvard's winter break in 1860 and has made a ghostly return. *Courtesy of the Library of Congress.*

Creepy pictures shot at Memorial Hall back up Shakespeare's conjecture. One photo, shot in early October 2012 and submitted to Cambridge Haunts, captured a spirit photo of what looks like a man from the Civil War era. He's wearing period garb and sporting facial hair indicative of the mid-1800s. The image is dark yellow in color, and Shakespeare believes it's of one of the Southern students who left during Harvard's winter break in 1860–61 during President Cornelius Conway Felton's stint. Most of the students who left that winter never returned.

In 1929, a proctor reported seeing a ghostly student in his Memorial Hall classroom. According to the teaching assistant, the full-bodied apparition would diligently fill out a blue book. "Just as the throng about the desk was greatest, he [the TA] caught a glimpse of the strange face. It was only a glimpse, and before he could say a word it was lost in the crowd," the *Harvard Crimson* reported in 1929. The mystery student was known as the Memorial

Hall ghost, and the so-called spirit kept returning to class to finish his exam… even though he was long gone.

In addition to its ghost lore, there are a few tall tales regarding the structure's gothic, red brick tower, which was destroyed in 1956. According to legend, the Cambridge Fire Department wanted to build a contemporary-style fire station in the triangle across from Memorial Hall. The department was told by the university's administration that its design would clash with the other buildings. However, Harvard secretly wanted that spot for Burr Hall. So when the fire of 1956 broke out, the firemen watched the Memorial Hall tower burn from across the street and told passersby that they didn't have enough water pressure to reach the blaze. After a forty-three-year absence, the tower was rebuilt in 1999.

Also, administrators have spotted odd objects dangling from the building's massive tower. Thomas E. Crooks, a former assistant to the dean from the class of '49, said he spotted jack-o'-lanterns hanging from the gargoyles atop the tower of Memorial Hall. "How in God's name did those pumpkins get up there?" Crooks told the *Crimson* in 1986. "I've heard tales that one of our mountaineering boys who passed on might have done it, but of course I don't have proof."

Or it could have been the workings of one of the seventy-one Confederate soldiers who died in battle. Perhaps the Memorial Hall ghost is making a postmortem plea, begging the living for inclusion among his Union soldier peers memorialized in the building's ornate, cross-shaped Transept.

File under: Confederate spirit

OLD POWDER HOUSE

The ominous stone tower overlooking the six-way intersection at Somerville's Nathan Tufts Park was initially built as a windmill by John Mallet in 1703 and then transformed into a powder magazine. In 1774, the British governor, Thomas Gage, confiscated the 250 barrels of gunpowder stored in the round structure so that the ammunition wouldn't be used by the American Patriots during the Revolutionary War. Musket-toting colonists—ticked off by Gage's orders to steal the powder—made their way to Cambridge, ready to fight. According to *Somerville, Past and Present*, an estimated fifty thousand armed men from across the colonies responded to the word-of-mouth alarm.

Resting on a hill and a stone's throw from Tufts University, the Old Powder House in Somerville has a colorful and allegedly haunted history that can be traced back to before the Revolutionary War. *Courtesy of the Library of Congress.*

Resting on a hill a stone's throw from Tufts University, the Old Powder House has a colorful and allegedly haunted history that can be traced back to before the war. Included in this back story are sightings of a cranky old spirit that haunts the mill on windy nights and spews curse words at passersby. In addition to the foul-mouthed apparition, reports suggest that some kind of residual energy of past trauma exists in the form of a phantom ball of blue sparks.

Why is the ghost so angry? According to Charles Skinner in *Myths and Legends of Our Own Land*, the old mill was the site of a tragic love story. Apparently, a penniless Somerville farmer and his girlfriend, the daughter of a wealthy landowner, once used the stone structure as a regular meeting place. One night, the father followed his daughter to her secret love nest. The maiden hid at the top of the mill to avoid her pops. She grabbed a rope to shimmy up the structure and somehow managed to set off the windmill's machinery. Her father's arm was accidentally severed by the grinding millstone. The girl's lover arrived, and they carried her father home. The father's injuries were fatal. However, his spirit is rumored to live on at the Old Powder House.

"Before she could summon heart to fix the wedding day, the girl passed many months of grief and repentance, and for the rest of her life, she avoided the old mill," wrote Skinner. "There was good reason for doing so, people said, for on windy nights, the spirits of the old man used to haunt the place, using such profanity that it became visible in the form of blue lights, dancing and exploding about the building."

Yep, the old man's ghost was cussing up a blue streak. There's also a contemporary retelling of the ghost story that involved a cross-dressing woman. "One version of the story tells of a young woman, dressed as a man, who sought refuge in the loft one night. But somehow a man who was up to no good discovered that she was actually a woman and tried to molest her," explained Cheri Revai in *Haunted Massachusetts*. "In the process, he became entangled in the mill's machinery and died. His restless spirit is said to still haunt the Powder House today."

Incidentally, the spirit's potty-mouthed antics continue to live on with hotheaded drivers and pedestrians trying to navigate the six-lane rotary in front of the haunted sentinel. In fact, Powderhouse Circle has the claim to fame of having the most motor-vehicle collisions in Somerville based on statistics collected by the city's SomerStat group. Massachusetts drivers? Now that's scary.

File under: blue lights

CHAPTER 6

NIGHTLIFE HAUNTS

Cambridge boasts a motley crew of nightlife locales rumored to be stomping grounds for spirits…and not the kind that come in a chilled martini glass. The list includes a bevy of atypical haunts, ranging from a former theater where diehards reenacted scenes from *The Rocky Horror Picture Show* to a regular from beyond at Cambridge Queen's Head pub. Apparently, the living aren't the only things that go bump in the nightlife.

Historically, Cambridge's watering holes were gathering places for Revolutionary-era Patriots and were, in essence, "nerve centers for spreading vital news and sanctuaries for outlawed organizations," wrote Roxie Zwicker in *Haunted Pubs of New England*. "Certain pubs bore witness to ghastly deeds and sorrowful tragedies," Zwicker continued. "Some of them became tinged with the aura of the supernatural."

British general John Burgoyne, who retreated with his troops after losing the Battle of Saratoga in 1777, was sent to Cambridge as a prisoner of war. However, no one wanted to take him in as a boarder, so he was forced to set up shop at the Blue Anchor Tavern, a popular gathering spot near Winthrop Park in Harvard Square, before convincing Cambridge's leaders to move him into the more plush Apthorp House. They granted the general his wish, but he was forced to buy his own furniture and pay rent. Apparently, his dislike of his living arrangements carried over to the afterlife. "Legend has it that Burgoyne's ghost still haunts the house," confirmed Harvard's Adams House. "Like many subsequent tenants in Cambridge, he complained bitterly about the lack of furnishings and the exorbitant rent he was forced to pay."

This historic photo of Harvard Square captures the ghosts of Cambridge's past. The Wadsworth House, the only surviving pre–Revolutionary War building facing Harvard Square, stands as a solemn reminder of when Cambridge was an agricultural town of farms, orchards and meadows. *Courtesy of the Library of Congress.*

In Cambridge's Central Square, the ghosts are less concerned with the furniture and a bit more rock-and-roll. Clay Fernald, the publicity and promotions manager at the Middle East, said the nightclub has become a rocker haunt of sorts for an important figure associated with the nightlife hot spot. In fact, the ashes of Billy Ruane, a longtime supporter of the Boston music scene and the man responsible for bringing live music to the Middle East in the 1980s, are enshrined in a spot above the bar. "Billy lives five feet away from my head," Fernald said, adding that he has continued to communicate with Ruane on a regular basis since his passing in November 2010. "I often turn around and see him at the corner of my eye," Fernald admitted. "I sometimes ask, 'Billy, what would you do?' when it comes to booking new acts or making major decisions. He doesn't always respond," Fernald mused, "but his energy is definitely still here."

One of the featured nightlife haunts, the Somerville Theatre, surrounds a former movie theater turned parking lot that has an odd history of mysterious fires. The empty lot, which is being converted into a luxury boutique hotel in Davis Square, is located at Day and Herbert Streets and had a cursed history as the former West Somerville Congregational Church turned Olympia Theatre (which was renamed Loews Davis Square movie theater) before it completely burned down in May 1942. On November 25, 1916, hundreds of children marched out of the building when a small fire was caused by a spark from the chimney. No one was hurt. In 1925, the scene was more traumatic. "Two women fainted in the crush and three other young women collapsed in the arms of their escorts on reaching the street," reported the *Globe*. "A piece of the highly inflammable film caught fire and immediately there was a lively blaze."

In June 1926, a third fire at the Olympia Theatre on Day Street turned deadly. Peter Neary, a projectionist from Lawrence, was burned alive. "Rolls of celluloid film were ignited and burned with great heat and bright flame," reported the *Globe*. "Only the fireproof construction of the room saved the entire balcony and gallery from the flames." The movie operator, who became a human torch, died in the hospital. There was a fourth fire on December 13, 1934. Not surprisingly, the movie house was completely destroyed by a blaze in 1942.

Cursed theater? Perhaps. Paranormal experts like Adam Berry from *Ghost Hunters* believe that the residual energy from the series of fires may have left a supernatural imprint on the buildings surrounding the old theater. "Anytime there's a traumatic event, it could be left behind." So it should come as no surprise that some of the area's nightlife haunts are a few steps away from a movie theater with a tragic history involving inexplicable sparks. *Night of the Living Dead*…anyone?

CAMBRIDGE QUEEN'S HEAD

In the bowels of Memorial Hall is Harvard's version of Harry Potter's the Three Broomsticks and the Leaky Cauldron. Instead of the Hogsmeade-style butterbeer, Cambridge Queen's Head pub serves up its frothy, signature homebrew called 1636, a draught beer supplied and developed exclusively for the nightlife hot spot by the Harpoon Brewery. Like Potter's magical hangouts boasting wayward wizards, muggles and death eaters, Cambridge's Queen's Head exudes a similar, otherworldly mystique.

In fact, patrons—limited, by the way, to Harvard alumni, students and their friends—are greeted by a spooky bronze gargoyle that fell off the building's tower during a blaze that destroyed the whole spire on September 6, 1956. Apparently, the eerie relic was missing in action for twelve years before ending up at the Fogg Museum. The gargoyle, whose open mouth was originally crafted to spew rainwater, is on loan and is displayed above the old-school bar area. It also serves as an ominous sentinel of the school spirits allegedly haunting the 1870s-era Gothic structure, which was built to commemorate the Harvard-bred students who died during the Civil War.

Sharing its name with a historic Southwark, England tavern bequeathed by the university's namesake, John Harvard, upon his death, Cambridge Queen's Head is a ringside seat to one of Cambridge's most reputedly haunted corridors. "The building is electric, and you can feel the energy when you're entering the pub," says Hank Fay, a tour guide with Cambridge Haunts and local musician who regularly performs at the campus haunt. "When we're loading equipment in the area behind Queen's Head, the back of my hair stands up. There's definitely something strange going on in that building."

For years, Memorial Hall's lower-level area was primarily used for storage and mechanical space. Opened in 2007 in Loker Commons, the pub had a past life as an animal laboratory for noted psychologist B.F. Skinner beginning in the 1940s through 1964. Skinner, who mainly experimented with pigeons and rats, invented the operant conditioning chamber, also known as the Skinner Box. In addition to the scientist's controversial approach to "radical" behaviorism, the Loker Commons area also hosted top-secret research for war-era combat vehicles and aircraft.

One employee who works in the building believes there's an inexplicable energy, or a supernatural imprint, left on the space. "Sometimes it feels like somebody or something walks by and there's nobody there," he said. "It's like when somebody walks by and you feel the air move. Sometimes late at night, it feels like there is somebody standing behind you. It's so bizarre."

The source, who wishes to remain anonymous, said the area directly above Cambridge Queen's Head is the building's most active spot for alleged paranormal activity. "I like to think it was a former student, possibly one of the Civil War soldiers the building was built for," he said. "Because Annenberg Hall has always been a dining hall, it could be a

Built in 2007, Cambridge Queen's Head pub is home to a gargoyle salvaged from the Memorial Hall fire of 1956 and serves Harvard students and at least one spirited regular allegedly lingering from the Civil War era. *Photo by Ryan Miner.*

chef or somebody who is in between worlds and is transitioning. I think the spirit is stuck and doesn't know which way to go," he said, adding that his friend who is a spiritualist confirmed that the area directly above Cambridge Queen's Head is indeed haunted.

During a recent tour of Annenberg Hall and Cambridge Queen's Head, there was definitely an inexplicable energy emanating from the area behind the pub while it was closed during Harvard's summer break. In fact, a *Ghosts of Cambridge* photographer captured a series of green-colored orbs surrounding the gargoyle rescued from Memorial Hall's pre-fire tower. According to paranormal experts, a green orb signals a friendly and communicative spirit.

However, as Adam Berry from *Ghost Hunters* pointed out, most so-called orbs captured in photos are mere light anomalies. "Most of the time it's just dust or insects," he explained. "The definition of an orb is a spherical object that produces its own light. So a real orb is created naturally by energy, or in theory, it's a spirit floating through and trying to show itself to you."

Ashley Shakespeare, a tour guide with Cambridge Haunts and sensitive to the paranormal world, said the area above Cambridge Queen's Head is definitely haunted by a Civil War–era student. According to the performer, the left-behind ghost "was one of the students from Harvard who fought in the Civil War and ended up being killed in battle never being able to return and finish his education," Shakespeare said. "He wanted to leave a legacy, but his life was taken away abruptly." Why would the soldier spirit linger at Cambridge Queen's Head pub? "They want to partake in the fun as well," he continued. "The spirits don't want to be left out."

Last call at Cambridge Queen's Head pub? Perhaps. Apparently, ghosts like their spirits too…downing a few of the pub's signature 1636 beer served in a silver mug. Bottoms up!

File under: barstool vortex

HARVARD SQUARE THEATER

The show must go on—even in the afterlife. Talk to anyone who has worked backstage at a theatrical venue, and they'll have a story or two of a close encounter with a playhouse phantom. For some reason, spirits love a good show, and Harvard Square's five-screen theater had a few silver-scream moments during its eighty-seven-year run.

So it was a sad day for film buffs and creep-show enthusiasts when the AMC Loews Harvard Square 5 closed its doors in late 2012. Home to the midnight showing of the cult classic *The Rocky Horror Picture Show* for twenty-eight years, the old-school movie house was originally built in 1925 as the University Theater. Its marquee and entrance faced Massachusetts Avenue and was later moved to Church Street in 1982. In the 1970s, the five-screen theater hosted rock legends ranging from Bob Dylan and Joan Baez to Iggy Pop and The Clash. An impromptu performance by Bruce Springsteen in 1974 catapulted the rocker into the national spotlight thanks to a glowing review by music critic Jon Landau.

The theater was also allegedly home to a playful poltergeist. According to several former workers and regulars who frequented the movie theater, the space was haunted. "The ghost is supposedly a former employee who died in the bathroom," mused one source who requested anonymity. "I've seen what looked like shadow figures while walking down the long corridor to theater

A Harvard Square nightlife hot spot for eighty-seven years, the former Harvard Square Theater supposedly boasted a former employee who died in the bathroom. With plans to revamp the former space into a retail complex, the only "ghost" from its University Theater days is a faded, hand-painted advertisement peeking out from its brick façade on Church Street. *Photo by Ryan Miner.*

5 [which was the theater's former stage], and people have heard laughter when nobody was there." The source said the theater's poor lighting and general creepy ambiance could have fueled the ghostly rumors.

Or it could have been the sweet transvestite doing the "Time Warp Again" in the main theater.

Whatever was dredging up the spooky tales from the crypt, skeptics contend that the inexplicable noises often reported in sites such as the old University Theater can be attributed to shoddy acoustics. However, the mischievous spirits at the Harvard Square Theater reportedly shut down the film projector when they weren't happy with a flick. Apparently, Cambridge's undead film critics sure can be picky.

Paranormal investigators like Adam Berry from *Ghost Hunters* strongly believe that poltergeists, or intelligent spirits responsible for physical disturbances like turning lights on and off, aren't bound to a specific location. For the record, the theater is a block away from Cambridge's Old Burying Ground and close to several of Cambridge's Revolutionary War–era haunts. Perhaps the AMC Loews Harvard Square 5 ghosts were just stopping in for a movie?

Speaking of the Revolutionary War, the University Theater's missing-in-action asbestos curtain featured a stunning rendition of George Washington taking command of the Continental army in 1775. The thirty-seven-foot-wide and seventeen-foot-tall oil rendering was painted by artist Claxton Byron Moulton and went missing in the late 1960s. "It could be in a barn in Minnesota or almost anywhere," responded the theater's former manager, Kevin Graham, when asked about the long-lost decorative oil painting.

In addition to its missing asbestos curtain, the former Harvard Square Theater had a history of riots involving college kids. In 1927, approximately forty Harvard students were arrested after a ruckus at a midnight show. "About 1:30 a.m. the students left the theater in a body and, 300 strong, poured into Harvard Square," reported the *Boston Globe* on February 12, 1927. "There they formed into a platoon and, with cheerleaders mounted on top of autos parked in the square, started making the early morning ring with Harvard cheers." Five students and one police officer were hurt in the mêlée.

Whether the AMC Loews Harvard Square 5 is indeed haunted is up for debate. However, there's no denying its historical significance as a theatrical venue. After officially closing its doors in late 2012, developers started revamping the space, transforming it into a retail complex. Meanwhile, enthusiasts can still spot a real ghost from the old haunt's University Theater days—a faded, hand-painted advertisement peeking out from the rooftop on Church Street. Yep, the former theater's brick façade still has its original University Theater ghost sign reminding passersby of the neighborhood movie house's glory days...or is it gory days?

File under: creep show

SOMERVILLE THEATRE

If the ominous red-eyed owls peering from the historic Somerville Theatre's marquee and peeking out from the labyrinthine hallways aren't enough to give you the chills, then its ghost lore involving a 1920s-era flapper will have your hair standing on end. Yep, the show must go on— even in the afterlife.

Built in 1914 by the Boston-based firm Funk & Wilcox, the Somerville Theatre was originally designed for stage shows, opera, vaudeville and, eventually, motion pictures. Before the Depression, the building boasted a basement café, bowling alley, billiards hall and the Hobbs Crystal Ballroom, a large dance space on the second floor that could easily host up to seven hundred foxtrotting partygoers. During its vaudeville heyday in 1915, the stage had its own stock company, the Somerville Theatre Players, and welcomed future icons like Tallulah Bankhead, Francis X. Bushman and Ray Bolger, who played the Scarecrow in MGM's *The Wizard of Oz*. Kay Corbett, who was part of the vaudeville-era sister act known as the Corbett Revue, also regularly appeared.

Apparently, the schedule was grueling for the Somerville Players. They launched a new play each week and performed twice a day. "We rehearse every morning from nine till twelve and then lunch, then a matinee every day, then dinner, then evening performances," wrote Bankhead in a letter to her grandfather dated 1919. "I'm nearly dead now and I have only been here a week."

For its grand opening on May 11, 1914, the one-thousand-plus-seat auditorium showcased a bevy of live acts, including the Stewart Sisters, a comedy skit from the Fuller-Rose company called *A King for a Day*, singing by the Adairs and a two-reel film presentation of *The Inventor's Wife*. Joseph Hobbs, who leased and eventually sold the theater to Arthur F. Viano in 1926, hired an up-and-comer and future film director Busby Berkeley, who went on to produce a slew of stylish musicals including

Built in 1914 for stage shows, opera, vaudeville and eventually motion pictures, the Somerville Theatre reportedly is home to a 1920s-era flapper who hangs around rows J and K in the orchestra-right section of the main theater. *Photo by Ryan Miner.*

42nd Street. The entertainment complex was a featured stop for seventeen years until the Depression's economic tumult forced it to be a movies-only establishment in 1932.

It's around this time that a ghost from its vaudeville past returned to claim her favorite seats in the main auditorium. "The story which has been told to me by two different unrelated sources is that there's an apparition around rows J and K in the orchestra-right section of the main theater here, which was built for movies and vaudeville in 1914," said Ian Judge, director of operations at the Somerville Theatre. "Some have seen her, and others have just seen the chair cushions in that section move. Those that have seen the ghost say that she resembles a woman from the 1920s or a flapper."

Judge, who eventually got validation about the haunting from a former office manager and a previous lessee, Galen Daly, said he had a close encounter with the flapper ghost when he first started his job more than one decade ago. "While I have never seen an apparition, I did see the seats move in a hard-to-explain way," Judge told the author. "I was doing some cleaning and renovation work overnight in the balcony. I was all alone, not another person in the building. As I was cleaning, I heard the sound of the seat cushions moving, as if someone were bouncing them up and down... they fold up, as theater seats often do. I rushed to the edge of the balcony and looked down and saw two of the seat cushions moving up and down, and they came to a stop as I watched. There was nobody else there, and nobody went out any of the exit doors."

The director of operations said he hadn't heard any stories about the flapper ghost until years after his close encounter. "I've never experienced anything since then, even though I've been alone here hundreds of times," Judge said. "I guess perhaps it was just the ghost welcoming me to my new job."

So, why haunted theaters? Holly Nadler, author of *Ghosts of Boston Town*, believes it's the romantic aesthetic. "All old and beautiful theaters look haunted, with their shadowy corridors, flickering lanterns, vaulted ceilings and Gothic ornaments," she wrote. "They also sound haunted, from the creaking of the woodwork, the rustling of old pipes, the sighs of air currents trapped inside thick stone walls. And indeed, there are some who contend that all old and beautiful theaters really are haunted."

A 1920s-era ticket seller, Sallie B. Irish, committed suicide by jumping out of her apartment in 1923. Perhaps Irish has made a postmortem return to her favorite seats in the Somerville Theatre's main stage? *Photo by Ryan Miner.*

Judge, among the believers, said he's still spooked. However, he has no clue who or what haunts the Somerville Theatre. "I don't know," he said when asked about the ghost's identity. "While nobody has ever died here that we know of, perhaps those were her favorite seats? Back in the days when we also had a stock theater company performing on stage around the movie season, people likely had reserved or favorite seats. Maybe she was a matinee-idol fan?"

One theory involves a former ticket seller, a die-hard fan of the Somerville Theatre and regular attendee of the stock theater company until she lost her vision. Sallie B. Irish, twenty-eight years old, committed suicide by jumping out of a fourth-story window in the Back Bay on May 10, 1923. "She had a nervous breakdown, involving trouble with her eyes, since which time she had worked [at the Somerville Theatre] only occasionally," reported the *Boston Daily Globe*. Irish apparently loved the theater and became hysterical when she started having vision problems. She was found dead on Massachusetts Avenue after jumping from her bedroom window. "Miss Irish was very popular about the Somerville Theatre and with its patrons, having worked there eight years," the *Globe* continued.

Perhaps Irish has made a postmortem return to her favorite seats in the main theater? Yes, all the world's a stage…and all of the lingering spirits are merely players.

File under: paranormal playhouse

SOURCES

The material in this book is drawn from published sources, including issues of the *Boston Globe, Daily Globe, Boston Herald, Boston Phoenix, New York Times* and college newspapers like the *Harvard Crimson* and *Harvard Gazette*. Several books on Cambridge's paranormal history were used and cited throughout the text. Other New England–based websites and periodicals, like CambridgeDay.com, *Yankee* and *Boston Spirit*, served as sources. I also conducted firsthand interviews, and some of the material is drawn from my own research. My first book, *Ghosts of Boston: Haunts of the Hub*, served as the primary source, and some of the material is updated in *Ghosts of Cambridge*. My Harvard Square ghost tour, Cambridge Haunts, also was a major source and generated original content. It should be noted that ghost stories are subjective, and I have made a concerted effort to stick to the historical facts, even if it resulted in debunking an alleged encounter with the paranormal.

Andrews, Joseph L. *Revolutionary Boston, Lexington, and Concord*. Beverly, MA: Commonwealth Editions, 2002.

Baltrusis, Sam. *Ghosts of Boston: Haunts of the Hub*. Charleston, SC: The History Press, 2012.

Balzano, Christopher. *Haunted Objects: Stories of Ghost on Your Shelf*. Iola, WI: Krause Publications, 2012.

Bunting, Bainbridge, and Robert H. Nylander. *Survey of Architectural History in Cambridge*. Cambridge, MA: Cambridge Historical Commission & MIT Press, 1973.

Dudley, Dorothy. *Theatrum Majorum: The Cambridge of 1776.* Whitefish, MT: Kessinger Publishing, 2007.

Fiedel, Dorothy Burtz. *Ghosts and Other Mysteries.* Ephrata, PA: Science Press, 1997.

Forest, Christopher. *Boston's Haunted History: Exploring the Ghosts and Graves of Beantown.* Atglen, PA: Schiffer Publishing, 2008.

Hauk, Dennis William. *Haunted Places: The National Directory.* New York: Penguin Group, 1996.

Hugh, Howard. *Houses of the Founding Fathers.* New York: Artisan, 2007.

Ketchum, Richard. *The World of George Washington.* N.p., n.d.

Kleespies, Gavin W., and Michael Kenney. *Rediscovering the Hooper-Lee-Nichols House.* Cambridge, MA: Cambridge Historical Society, 2010.

Mont, Joseph, and Marcia Weaver. *Ghosts of Boston.* Boston: Snakehead Press, 2002.

Nadler, Holly Mascott. *Ghosts of Boston Town: Three Centuries of True Hauntings.* Camden, ME: Down East Books, 2002.

Penzler, Otto. *The Big Book of Ghost Stories.* New York: Vintage Books, 2012.

Rapaport, Diane. *The Naked Quaker: True Crimes and Controversies.* Beverly, MA: Commonwealth Editions, 2007.

Revai, Cheri. *Haunted Massachusetts: Ghosts and Strange Phenomena of the Bay State.* Mechanicsburg, PA: Stackpole Books, 2005.

Rooney, Ashley E. *Cambridge, Massachusetts: Ghosts, Legends & Lore.* Atglen, PA: Schiffer Publishing, 2009.

Rule, Leslie. *When the Ghost Screams: True Stories of Victims Who Haunt.* Kansas City, MO: Andrews McMeel Publishing, 2006.

Swayne, Matthew. *America's Haunted Universities: Ghosts That Roam Hallowed Halls.* Woodbury, MN: Llewellyn Wordwide, 2012.

Tucker, Elizabeth. *Haunted Halls: Ghostlore of American College Campuses.* Jackson: University Press of Mississippi, 2007.

Zwicker, Roxie J. *Haunted Pubs of New England: Raising Spirits of the Past.* Charleston, SC: The History Press, 2007.

ABOUT THE AUTHOR

Journalist Sam Baltrusis, author of *Ghosts of Boston: Haunts of the Hub*, freelances for various publications, including *Boston Spirit* magazine, and is the managing editor of *Scout Magazines* in Somerville and Cambridge. He has been featured as Boston's paranormal expert on the Biography Channel's *Haunted Encounters* and *Paranormal State*'s Ryan Buell's *Paranormal Insider Radio*. He moonlights as a tour guide and produces Harvard Square's Cambridge Haunts ghost tour, highlighting the city's historical haunts. He's also a sought-after lecturer who speaks at dozens of paranormal-related events scattered throughout New England. In the past, he's worked for VH1, MTV.com, *Newsweek*, WHDH.com and ABC Radio and as a regional stringer for the *New York Times*.

Author Sam Baltrusis signs copies of his first book, *Ghosts of Boston: Haunts of the Hub*, at an allegedly haunted location in Provincetown, Massachusetts. The half-scale replica of the *Rose Dorothea* schooner in the Provincetown Library is rumored to be haunted by Captain Marion Perry, who won the Lipton Cup in August 1907. *Photo by Christian Parker.*